THE GREAT REBELLION

THE PATH OF LIBERATION FROM SUFFERING

Samael Aun Weor

GLORIAN
2009

The Great Rebellion
A Glorian Book / 2009
Fifth Edition (English)

Originally published as "La Gran Rebelión," 1976

This Edition © 2009 Glorian Publishing

ISBN 978-1-934206-22-5
Library of Congress Control Number: 2006908904

Glorian Publishing is a non-profit organization.
For more information, visit our websites:

glorian.info
gnosticbooks.org
gnosticteachings.org
gnosticradio.org

Contents

ULTAN
Enjoy
JFK.

"It is necessary to be in a receptive attitude, in the Buddhist style, that is, with the bowl facing up, waiting for psychological nourishment..."

Introduction

In the world there exist many orators and writers who amaze others with their eloquence; however, to know how to listen to the word is something extremely difficult since indeed, few are they who know how to listen to the word.

The audience might be attentively following the words of the speaker or the readers might be attentively following the words of the writer. They might be listening and focused; however, within their psychological depth there exists a secretary who translates the words of the speaker or of the writer. That secretary is the "I," the myself, the ego. That secretary usually misinterprets or mistranslates the articulated or written words.

The "I" translates the word according to its prejudgments, pre-conceptions, fears, pride, anxieties, ideas, etc.

The readers of a book or the people in an auditorium are certainly not listening to the words of the author, instead they are listening to themselves. They are listening to their own ego; they hear their beloved Machiavellic ego, which is incapable of understanding the real, the true, the essential.

Only in a state of alert novelty, with a spontaneous mind, without the weight of the past, in a state of complete receptiveness can we really listen to the words without the intervention of that bad secretary called the "I," the myself, the ego.

A mind that is conditioned by the memory only repeats what it has stored. A mind, conditioned by the experiences of so many yesterdays, can only see the present through the dirty glasses of the past.

Therefore, if we want to learn how to listen to the word in order to discover the new, then it is urgent to learn how to live from moment to moment without the preoccupations of the past and without the projections of the future. We must live accordingly with the philosophy of momentariness.

The truth is the unknowable from moment to moment. If we want to be completely receptive our minds must be attentive always, in complete attention, without prejudgments and preconceptions.

┴ It is necessary to learn how to live wisely, to refine our senses, to refine our behavior, thoughts and feelings.

Of what use is to have a great academic culture if indeed we do not know how to listen to the word, if we are not capable of discovering the new from moment to moment.

Rough, rude, deteriorated and degenerated minds can never know how to discover the new. These types of minds only mistakenly recognize the absurd translations of that secretary called "I," the ego, the myself.

Fanatics of Marxism-Leninism do not accept the new; they do not admit the fourth characteristic of everything, that is, the Fourth Coordinate because of their self-esteem, because they love themselves too much, because they are confined to their own absurd theories. Thus, when we place them upon the field of concrete facts, when we demonstrate to them how absurd their sophisms are then they raise their left arm, look at their watch, excuse themselves and leave.

So, degenerated minds, decrepit minds do not know how to listen to the word. They do not know how to discover the new; they do not accept reality because they are bottled up within their self-esteem. They are people who love themselves too much; they do not know anything about cultural refinements because rough and rude minds only listen to their beloved ego.

First of all it is necessary to learn how to listen to the word. Indeed, those who know how to read the written word are very rare. Normally, when somebody is reading, in reality, he is not listening to the word because his "I," his ego is translating what he reads into his own language, into his own particular idiosyncrasy, into his own criterion.

First of all, we must awaken our consciousness in order to learn how to listen to the word. How could somebody whose consciousness is asleep be capable of listening psychologically?

In order to know how to listen psychologically, it is necessary to be present, so I ask you: In this moment are you sure that you are not mentally wandering somewhere else, perhaps in a workshop, or in the countryside or in some other place?

When people read a Gnostic book or when they are seated listening to a lecture, they seem to be listening to the word; however, if they are not psychologically present, if they are not consciously in their home (physical body), how are they able to listen to the word?

Normally, when one teaches Gnosis, people seem to be listening but in fact they are not listening; they are escaping, they are mentally walking from here to there, from there to here; they are traveling within their own inner psychological city.

Let us remember that within each one of us there exists a psychological country. One thing is the physical city where we live and another thing is the psychological city within which we are psychologically situated.

Where are you psychologically situated at this moment? You might say 'here' but that might or might not be right. The truth is that it is difficult to know how to listen to the word. Normally the person who is listening escapes, travels within his own psychological country and runs away in different directions. So, if the person's consciousness is not at home (his physical body), if his psyche is not at home, who is listening then? The human personality? Indeed, the human personality does not know how to listen. Perhaps the physical body is listening? But the physical body is a mere instrument!

When one speaks to other people, one thinks that they are alert; however, they are only apparently listening because they are not at home psychologically.

They are so full of themselves that they do not want to listen to the word. Within themselves they do not have an empty place, a small corner for the word; they are full of vanity, pride, full of their own theories, etc. How could the word enter within them if they are so full of themselves?

Let us remember Jesus and his birth (in the time of Herod) when his parents went to be taxed and there was no room for them in the inn. So, within the inn (our interior), there was no empty space for the word. Our inn is always full; our psychological inn is always full. How serious this is indeed!

We have to have Buddha's small bowl always facing up in order to receive the word; however, instead, people do the contrary; they put their bowl turned down. It is necessary to recognize our own inner misery in order to have a place for the word within our small bowl, within our mind.

But if we are so full of ourselves, how could the word enter within us? In other words, how could we learn how to listen from a psychological point of view? Because to know how to physically listen is something relatively easy, but to listen psychologically is indeed difficult!

It is necessary to be in a receptive attitude, in the Buddhist style, that is, with the bowl facing up, waiting for psychological nourishment; but if the bowl is turned down, how could the psychological nourishment enter within us? How could we receive it?

Those who are full of pride, of self-sufficiency, those who are full of theories, are they perhaps in the correct psychological state to receive the word? First of all, we have to recognize our own misery and inner poverty before receiving the nourishment of the word; however, it is not possible to receive that nourishment if we do not know how to listen to the word.

It so happens that we have read or listened to the word thousands or even millions of times; therefore, we believe that we know it, that we have listened to it or comprehended it; but as a matter of fact, we have not listened to the word at all. On any given day, we listen to the word again and we feel that there is something new. Why do we feel that there is something new? Because we always read or listened with our consciousness asleep, and on the other day we had the luck of listening while in a state of awakened consciousness.

Understand how difficult it is to know how to listen. First of all, it is necessary to be self-cognizant if we want to know how to listen.

Let us remember the temptation of Jesus when the devil said to him: *All these things will I give thee, if thou wilt fall down and worship me.*

Let us understand the temptation: Jesus Christ was asked to put his bowl facing down, in order to listen to external things, in order to listen to the world only with the external senses; he was not asked to put his bowl facing up, which is the way to receive the inner word that comes from the heights.

So, why did Jesus not fall? Because he was always alert and vigilant as the watchman in times of war; he had his small bowl (mind) facing up. However, if he would have fallen into temptation, that is, if he would have put his small bowl, his mind facing down, he would have listened to the external words, the things that come from outside, the things of the world; he would not have been able to listen psychologically.

So dear reader, we have to become more receptive to the written words; we have to learn to listen psychologically. I repeat, how could it be possible to listen if we are outside of our house? Who are they that are outside of their house? They are all of the unconscious ones!

Are you sure that you are listening now? Can you affirm it? Can you be assured that you are totally attentive? Or, are you wandering in other places? The crude reality of the facts is that when people listen, they do not know how to listen because they are always in other places; they are never at home.

People do not remember their past existences. How could it be possible for them to remember past existences if they are not at home? How could someone remember something that they have not yet experienced?

Do you know what it means to be at home? Psychologically, we understand that "'home" is the human person. Normally, one's Real Being is out of his house; then, how could we remember our past existences if we are out of our house all of the time?

In our Gnostic studies there are two primary things: first, to remember ourselves, that is, to remember our Real Being and second, the relaxation of the physical body. To remember the Self and to relax the body is something that we have to constantly do. Remember that the body, the nerves, the muscles are always in tension. It is imperative to learn how to remember the Self and to relax the body. I do it everyday, continuously, while in my bed or anywhere. To do these two primary things is something indispensable.

As a matter of fact, people make many mistakes; they have elaborated upon many complicated theories because they have forgotten their Real Being. For example, if Laplace, the great French astronomer and mathematician would not have forgotten himself, his own Real Being, he would not have conceived of his theory in his mind (the famous theory of Laplace). The theory of Laplace is false and absurd. When Laplace presented his theory to Napoleon Bonaparte, and explained to him how from a nebula, a planet or a solar system comes forth, Napoleon asked him: "And in which place did you put God in your theory?" Then Laplace answered cynically to Napoleon: "No sir, I did not need God to elaborate upon my theory;" observe Laplace's self-sufficiency.

Nonetheless, it is precisely because he forgot his Inner Being that he could create such a false theory. Presently, not a single astronomer from the planet Earth has seen with his own eyes a planet coming forth or emerging from a nebula. But incongruently, Laplace's theory is admitted as dogma by the minds of many fools. If Laplace would not have forgotten his Real Self, he would not have constructed such an absurd theory.

A fool put some drops of oil in a cup of water and with a small stick he swirled the drops of oil; the swirling produced rings that were rotating around the central drop. "Oh!" He exclaimed, "This is how the universe was formed!" Then he was asked: "And God?" He then answered: "No, God was not necessary; you can see in my theory how it was formed." Indeed, he was really a fool; he did not realize that when performing his theory with the drops of oil in a cup of water, he was playing the role of God; that as a God he was making the oil whirl.

Nevertheless, he was such a fool that he could not realize that somebody was needed in order to produce the movements of the oil with the stick, because the drop of oil by itself could not rotate or would not have spread and formed the rings. So, a hand was necessary and an intelligent impulse; so the cynic, the fool, was playing the role of God; however, he denied God. So, this is how torpid people are when they forget their Real Selves.

I do not forget my Real Self, that is, my Real Being; therefore, I state that Laplace's nebular theory is false. I will go further in this matter. I understand Sabaoth,[1] and Sababhath. What is Sababhath? It is the directive intelligence formed by Sabaoth, by the Army of the Voice.

How did the universe emerge? Did it come from a nebula? No! That theory is not true. The Universe came forth from Sabaoth, from the mother-substance, from the Chaos, from that which the Hindustanis call Mulaprakriti.

Tantric philosophy teaches the truth. It is stated that some Tantric rites were celebrated at the dawn of the Mahamanvantara (Cosmic Day). The Elohim which in their conjunction form Sabaoth, the Army of the Voice, unfolded themselves in the form of divine androgynous beings. Subsequently, when they took the form of male and female principles, they were ready to fecundate the chaotic matter. In this manner, Isis and her mas-

---

1 - Sabaoth (Hebrew, "tsebha'oth"): An army or host, from Saba, "to go to war." See Isa. 1.9; Rom. 9.29; James 5.4; translated in the Bible as "Lord of Hosts" or "Almighty."

culine principle Osiris, that is, Sabaoth, had a kind of chemical and metaphysical copulation in order to fecundate the chaotic matter.

This is how (within the chaos) they separated the superior waters from the inferior waters. The superior waters were fecundated by the fire (the masculine principle) and the cosmic fire ascended through the spinal column of Isis (Mulaprakriti); later that fire returned into the Chaos. So, this is how the Chaos was fecundated and this is how life appeared. This is how the bed seed of all that exists surged forth. The cause was, has been and always will be the electric whirlwind that generates life everywhere. Afterwards, the germs of existence, the elemental atoms, the planets with plenty of life, sprang forth. All of this thanks to Elohim; thanks to the divine androgynous or host of Elohim; not from a nebula!

The first form that came into existence was a Mental universe. Much later it crystallized into Astral matter, then after that into Ethereal matter and finally into physical matter. There was no nebula as Laplace had stated. The Universe was the creation of the Verb, the Word.

If Laplace would not have forgotten his Real Self, if instead of creating that foolish theory he would have worked deeply on meditation, then it is obvious that he would have one day seen (with the Dangma Eye) the real origins of the universe, a reality that is far away from his foolish theory. This is the crude reality of the facts!

So, when one forgets one's Real Self, one makes frightful mistakes. Therefore, what is fundamental is not to forget one's Real Self.

The fire is what counts in any creation; however, we are not referring to the fire in this physical world, but to the fire within the Chaos. Obviously, in the Chaos the fire is an electric potency with possibilities of awakening in order to create.

In my book *The Pistis Sophia Unveiled*, I state that Pistis Sophia is definitive within the Chaos. Indeed, Sophia is the wisdom of the fire that shines within the Chaos; this is why

1 - Dangma Eye: the clear vision of a purified soul, a Dangma (Sanskrit)

it is stated that "light comes forth from darkness" and that "the cosmos comes forth from the chaos." Pistis Sophia as fire shines within the Chaos in order to create and to create anew. The divine wisdom is within the Chaos and from the Chaos it comes forth in order to arrive to the "13th Aeon," to the "13th Serpent," to the "13th Numeral Seven."

So dear readers, we have to reflect more and more upon these psychological matters. Great truths are understood when one does not forget his Real Being, when one profoundly remembers the Self.

Therefore we recommend that you, our reader, remember your Self on a daily basis and relax your physical body completely on a sofa, just for a moment (whether it be for five or ten minutes, or for half an hour). Thus, one day you will be able to experience the reality within your consciousness. This practice brings the superior emotional center together with the motor center into activity; thus, when in complete relaxation, our consciousness experiences the Being, feeling Him, experiencing Him.

So, it is fundamental to become receptive to our Being. Our personality has to become more and more passive and receptive to the Word that comes from the heights; that word comes through the superior centers of the Being; this is how the Word arrives. However, if we are not receptive, if we do not learn how to relax our bodies, if we forget our Selves, how could we receive the messages that come forth through the superior centers of our Being?

Our readers have to comprehend that we have to become receptive; that it is necessary to learn to receive the word and to capture its profound meaning. We have to relax and remember ourselves, our own Being daily; in this way we will successfully advance.

Is it not useless for a student to ask a Master for counsel when the student is not in self-remembrance, since he will be unable to listen?

Well, to ask for counsel is necessary but to know how to listen is indispensable. So, it is not absurd to ask for counsel; what is absurd is to not know how to listen to the word.

Is it possible to learn how to listen through the education of the word? One thing is to speak it or write it and another thing is to listen to the word. If we do not know how to listen to the word, we will not grasp the true knowledge.

In order to know how to listen, it is necessary to stay psychologically alert and on guard, to be cognizant. The existence of a total balance between knowledge and comprehension or between knowledge and the Being is also necessary. However, one thing is to listen to the word and another thing is to speak the word. To educate the uttered word is convenient but to know how to listen to the word is indispensable.

When one is in front of an illuminated Master there is a lethargy of the mind; one is unable to absorb all of the words of the Master, the transcendental knowledge. One feels perplexed and stunned before the wisdom of the Master; so it is indeed hard to listen to an illuminated Master. So, what could we do in order to learn how to listen to a Venerable Master?

Undoubtedly, it is necessary to know how to listen to the word; it is necessary to be in the state of alert-perception, alert-novelty if one wants to grasp the true knowledge. However, I repeat, how could one know how to listen if one is not at home? Normally, the people that form the audience or who read a book escape, because they have multiple inhuman psychic aggregates that go and come everywhere. So, in an auditorium many people might be listening, but generally they are not remembering themselves; thus they are not listening; they do not listen because they are outside of their house. If one wants to know how to listen to the word, one needs to be integral, one needs to be complete, as a whole in front of the lecturer. The three brains: the Intellectual, the Emotional and the Motor have to be united, integrated, but if those three brains are disassociated, for example: the Intellectual is in one direction, the Emotional in another and the Motor in yet another, then, one is hearing but not listening to the word.

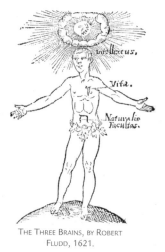

THE THREE BRAINS, BY ROBERT FLUDD, 1621.

So, to know how to read is to know how to listen to the word; it is something very difficult but fundamental, because if one learns it, then one can receive complete information about the Gnostic esoteric work.

Let us take into account that practical life has many faces. A life lived in an unconscious state has terrible faces. It seems that life as humanity lives it, that is, in an unconscious state has more power than the Gnostic esoteric knowledge has. Nevertheless, what happens is that they cannot receive the information given to them through the written or articulated word because people are so full of themselves; they are full of false knowledge that impedes them to receive the complete information; that is, they do not know how to listen.

If one is listening, if one learns how to listen in a state of alert-perception and alert-novelty, then through the word one can recognize that he or she is receiving knowledge because one is *nobody*. Then, there is an empty place within which the word can enter; but if one feels filled with knowledge, vain and satisfied with all of those know-it-all egos, how could one receive the word?

So, we have to put our urn, our small bowl facing up, open, waiting for the word, for the nourishment that will feed and orientate us. But if one turns the bowl down, how can he receive the knowledge? So to receive, it is necessary to put it facing up; to have a place in our minds in order to receive a drop, a drop of knowledge.

False education, false morality, is also an obstacle in order to learn how to listen. Certainly, false education produces a lot of damage. We state that the education that one receives in kindergarten, in elementary school, in high school and in university is false because it is not related with any of the autonomous and self-cognizant parts of the Being. It is false; therefore it distorts the five centers of the human machine and nourishes many inhuman psychic aggregates.

A person with a robust false personality is a person that is not disposed to listen to the word, because he does not know how to listen. A person with a robust false personality always listens to the subjective, infraconscious, infrahuman voices of the five centers of his organic machine. The only voices that he knows how to listen to are the voices of his false personality. He is always full of false knowledge and does not have an empty place wherein the instructor could deposit the word on high. So, false education produces a frightful narrow-mindedness.

Regarding false morals, it is good to know what kind of morals we are speaking about, because if these morals are attached to the old, to traditions, they are useless.

It is better if we speak about revolutionary ethics, because people's morals are slaves of their customs, places and epochs. What is moral in a country is immoral in another; what in one epoch was moral in another was immoral; what in one moment in time is moral is immoral in another.

Let us refer to an actual case. In China, up until not too long ago, to kill one's father because he was very old was looked upon as moral. Also, the exchange of little girls by catholic missionaries for (mail) stamps was seen as moral. There was a priest that bought hundreds, thousands of little girls that he acquired with mere stamps. It was also moral to throw a newborn girl into the street just because she was a female; but they felt happy when the newborn baby was a boy. So, what is morality? Morality is the slave of traditions. We could quote thousands of cases, some of them very painful and others even shameful when talking about the much boasted morality.

So, morality is the slave of customs, of times, of the prejudgments of humanity. Therefore, people's morality is not practical for the one who wants to walk on the path of the realization of the inner Being. One has to liberate himself from this type of morality in order to walk on the path of the great rebellion.

Let us talk about revolutionary ethics; that sounds better. One needs to do a psychological inventory of oneself in order to know what it is that one has in excess and what it is that one needs and also to learn how to handle virtues.

If a virtue is out of place (even if it is very holy) it produces damage. There have been many saints that have harmed humanity with their virtues; this is the crude reality of the facts. If one does not know how to use virtues, no matter how precious they might be, it is obvious that one generates damage with them. So, let us not talk about morality, instead let us talk about revolutionary ethics. Morality is useless; it damages our psychological development.

It is necessary to know how to listen and for that, one needs to be at home. But, what about our bad psychological secretary, the ego?

The egos of the people in the audience have already formed their own personal concepts according to their psychological idiosyncrasies even before the speaker has finished his lecture or before finishing a book. The ego forms false concepts because the latter are based on his prejudgments, fears, false theories, false education, etc., and many other "weeds." The ego is a bad secretary that produces a lot of damage. It is for this reason that it is necessary to be psychologically alert and vigilant if we want to be disposed to receive the word, always paying attention, always in rebellion against our ego, always in the present. Because, if we are absent, if we are not listening accordingly with the philosophy of momentariness, how could we receive the doctrine of the Being, that is, the doctrine of the great rebellion?

Inverential peace!

Samael Aun Weor

"The world has become terribly monotonous; everywhere there exist unchanging streets and appalling housing."

Chapter 1
Life

As incredible as it may sound, it is certainly true that this so-called modern civilization is frightfully ugly. It does not even fulfill the transcendental characteristics of aesthetics and is devoid of inner beauty.

We greatly boast of those conventional, horrifying structures that resemble the nests of rats.

The world has become terribly monotonous; everywhere there exist unchanging streets and appalling housing.

All this has become tiresome throughout the world, in the north, the south, the east and the west.

The same uniformity exists everywhere, horribly nauseating and sterile. "Modernization," exclaim the multitudes.

We resemble vain peacocks with our fine clothes and shiny shoes while here, there and everywhere are unhappy, undernourished and wretched millions.

Simplicity and natural beauty, spontaneous and genuine with no need for vain accessories and cosmetics, has disappeared in the female sex. Nowadays we are *modern*; such is life.

People have grown dreadfully cruel. There is a chill on kindness. Nobody has compassion for anyone anymore.

The display windows of luxury stores glisten with extravagant merchandise, which the less fortunate definitely cannot afford.

In our society those who are outcast can only gaze upon silks and jewels, costly bottles of perfume and umbrellas for downpours. They can look but they cannot touch, a torment similar to that of Tantalus.

The modern human being has become grossly rude. The perfume of friendship and the fragrance of sincerity have, for the most part, disappeared.

The teeming masses complain of being overtaxed; everyone has problems; someone owes us or we owe them; we are sued and have nothing with which to pay; worries ravage our brains; nobody lives in peace....

Bureaucrats sustain themselves psychologically upon their smugly curved paunches and fat cigars, while cunningly playing political mind games with absolutely no concern for people's suffering.

Nowadays, no one is happy, least of all those of the middle class who find themselves with their backs to the wall facing the sword.

Rich and poor, believers and nonbelievers, merchants and beggars, shoemakers and tinsmiths only live because they must. They drown their torments with wine and even become drug addicts to escape themselves.

People have become malicious, suspicious, distrustful, astute and perverse; no one believes in anyone anymore. Every day they invent new conditions, certificates, all kinds of restrictions, documents, credentials, etc., none of which serves a real purpose anymore. The astute mock all this nonsense: they do not pay; they evade the law even though they risk being hauled off to jail.

No job provides happiness. The sense of true love has been lost, and people are married today, divorced tomorrow.

Lamentably, family unity has been lost. There is no longer an innate sense of modesty. Lesbianism and homosexuality have become as common as drinking a glass of water.

The purpose of this book is certainly to find out more about all this, to try to understand the causes of such moral breakdown, to investigate, to seek.

I am speaking in an everyday, practical language in hopes of finding out what is hidden behind this horrible masquerade of existence.

I am thinking aloud, and let the swindlers of the intellect say whatever they please.

Theories have already become humdrum. They are even sold and resold in the marketplace... then what?

Theories serve only to worry us and embitter our lives.

Goethe rightly said, "Every theory is grey and only the tree of the golden fruits of life is green."

The wretched people are already weary of many theories. Nowadays they talk a great deal about being practical. We need to be practical and really come to know the causes of our sufferings.

"Beginning with the year 2000 it will be almost
impossible to find a beach where one can
swim in pure water."

Chapter 2
Harsh Reality

Soon millions of inhabitants of Africa, Asia, and South America may die of starvation.

Gases released from aerosol sprays could put an end to the ozone layer of the Earth's atmosphere.

Some experts forecasted that after the year two thousand the subsoil of our Earth will be exhausted.

It has already been proven that marine species are dying due to pollution of the sea.

Unquestionably, at this rate, by the end of this century all the inhabitants of large cities will have to wear oxygen masks to protect themselves from fumes.

If pollution continues at this alarming pace, before long it will be impossible to eat fish. Living in totally infected waters, fish will become a serious danger to our health.

Beginning with the year 2000 it will be almost impossible to find a beach where one can swim in pure water.

Due to excessive consumption and exploitation of the topsoil and subsoil, soon the land will be unable to produce the agricultural products necessary to feed the world.

By contaminating the oceans with so much waste, poisoning the air with fumes from cars and factories, destroying the Earth with underground atomic explosions and the excessive use of elements harmful to the Earth's crust, clearly the "'intellectual animal"—mistakenly called a human being—is subjecting the planet Earth to a long, appalling death, which will undoubtedly end in a great catastrophe.

It has been difficult for the world to cross the threshold of the year 2000 since the "'intellectual animal" is destroying the natural environment at breakneck speed.

The "rational mammal" mistakenly called the human being is intent on destroying the Earth, making it uninhabitable. Obviously, he is succeeding.

As far as the sea is concerned, the nations of the world have clearly changed it into some sort of huge dump.

Seventy percent of the entire world's waste is going into the sea.

Enormous quantities of oil, all kinds of insecticides, numerous chemical substances, poisonous and neurotoxic gases, detergents etc., are annihilating all the species that live in the oceans.

Sea birds and plankton—essential for life—are being destroyed. Without a doubt, the extermination of marine plankton is of incalculable severity, for it is this microorganism that produces 70 percent of the Earth's oxygen.

Scientific research has produced verifiable evidence that certain parts of the Atlantic and Pacific Oceans are polluted with the radioactive waste of atomic explosions.

In capital cities of the world, and especially in Europe, they drink a fresh type of water, then they eliminate it, purify it, and later drink it again. Drinking water goes through the human organism many times in large, "super-civilized" cities.

In the city of Cucuta, Colombia, near the Venezuelan border in South America, the inhabitants are obliged to drink the defiled water from the river that carries all the filth from the sewers of Pamplona. I am referring emphatically to the Pamplonita River, which has been such blight for the "Pearl of the North" (Cucuta). Fortunately, there is another aqueduct supplying water to the city, but people still have to drink the putrid water of the Pamplonita River.

Huge filters, gigantic machines and chemical substances attempt to purify the dirty waters of Europe's big cities. However, epidemics continue to break out because of the frequency with which this filthy waste water has passed through the human organism.

Famous bacteriologists have encountered all types of viruses, bacilli, pathogens, tubercular bacteria, typhus, small pox, larvae, etc., in the drinking water of all large capital cities.

Although it seems incredible, the poliomyelitis vaccine has been found in the water of treatment plants throughout Europe.

Moreover, the waste of water is shocking. Modern scientists have asserted that beginning with the year 1990 the "rational humanoid" will die of thirst.

Worst of all is that the underground fresh water reserves are endangered by the abuses of the "intellectual animal."

The merciless exploitation of oil wells continues to be fatal.Oil extracted from the Earth's interior gets filtered through the underground water routes, which then become contaminated. Consequently, for more than a century, oil has polluted the Earth's subterranean water supply.

Obviously, a result of all this has been the death of vegetation as well as a multitude of people.

Let us talk briefly about the air which is absolutely indispensable for the life of all creatures... With every breath, our lungs take in one tenth of a gallon of air, which amounts to 3,170 gallons per day. Multiply this quantity by the current population living on Earth, and we have an accurate amount of the daily intake of oxygen consumed by humanity. This does not take into account the oxygen consumption of all the other animals on the face of the Earth.

The total amount of oxygen we inhale is found in the atmosphere and comes from plankton, which we are now destroying with pollution, and also from vegetation photosynthesis. Unfortunately, the reserves of oxygen are being exhausted.

The "rational mammal"—mistakenly called a human being—through his innumerable industries, is constantly diminishing the Solar radiation essential for photosynthesis. For this reason the quantity of oxygen currently produced by plants is significantly less than it was in the last century.

The gravest world tragedy caused by the "intellectual animal" is that he continues to contaminate the sea, destroying plankton and exhausting the vegetation.

Regrettably, the "rational animal" proceeds to destroy his oxygen sources. The smog that the "rational humanoid" is constantly discharging into the air is lethal and is endangering the life of planet Earth.

Smog is not only exhausting the oxygen reserves, but it is also killing people. It has been shown that smog causes strange, dangerous, incurable illnesses. Smog impedes the entrance of sunlight and ultraviolet light, causing serious disorders in the atmosphere.

An era of climatic changes is approaching: glaciation, the advancement of polar ice toward the equator, terrifying cyclones, earthquakes, etc.

Beginning with the year 2000, some regions of the planet Earth will heat up, not because of the use of electrical energy, but because of its abuse. This will contribute to the revolution of the Earth's axis. Soon the poles will become the Earth's equator and the Equator will end up at the poles.

The poles have begun to thaw out and a new great flood is approaching, preceded by fire.

Forthcoming decades will see an increase in carbon dioxide, which will form a thick layer around the Earth's atmosphere. Unfortunately, such a filter or layer will absorb thermal radiation and cause a deadly Greenhouse Effect.

The Earth's climate will become warmer in many areas, and this will melt the polar ice caps, causing a shockingly rapid rise in the level of the oceans.

This is a very serious situation. While fertile soil is disappearing, two hundred thousand people who need to be fed are being born every day. Surely, the coming worldwide famine will be terrifying. It is already at our doorstep.

Nowadays, forty million people die of starvation every year because of a lack of food.

The criminal industrialization of the forest and the merciless exploitation of mines and oil wells are turning the Earth into a desert.

While it is certainly well-known that nuclear energy is fatal for humanity, the existence today of "death rays," "microbial bombs," and many other terribly destructive and malignant elements invented by scientists is no less certain.

Unquestionably, the production of nuclear energy requires vast amounts of potentially uncontrollable heat, which can cause a nuclear disaster at any time.

To obtain nuclear energy requires enormous quantities of radioactive minerals of which we use only 30 percent. This is rapidly exhausting the world's subsoil.

The atomic waste that is left in the ground is horribly dangerous. A safe method for the disposal of atomic waste simply does not exist.

If gases were to leak out from one of those atomic dumps, however minute the amount, thousands of people would die.

Contamination of food and water brings about genetic mutations and human monstrosities: creatures that are born deformed and abnormal.

A serious nuclear accident occurred before the year 1999 that caused real alarm.

Certainly humanity does not know how to live. It has degenerated terribly and, frankly, has sped towards the abyss.

Gravest of all these facts is that the factors of such desolation—starvation, wars, destruction of the planet on which we live, etc.—also exist within us. We carry all of these things inside, within our own psyche.

"People spend a lifetime looking for happiness
everywhere and die without ever finding it."

Chapter 3

Happiness

People work daily; they struggle to survive. Somehow they want to exist. However, they are not happy.

The word happiness is "Greek" to people, as we say around here. However, worst of all is that they know this. But amid so much bitterness, it seems they do not lose the hope of achieving happiness one day without knowing how or in what way.

Wretched people! They suffer so much! However, they want to live and are afraid of dying...

If people were to understand something about revolutionary psychology, they would possibly think differently; but the fact is that they do not know anything. What they want is to survive in the midst of their misfortune, and that is all.

There are pleasant and enjoyable moments, but this is not happiness. People confuse pleasure with happiness.

Parties, bar hopping, drinking sprees and orgies are brutish pleasures, but they are not happiness... There are, however, wholesome get-togethers without over-indulgence, vulgar behavior, and the abuse of alcohol. But that is not happiness either.

Are you a kind person? How do you feel when you dance? Are you in love? Is it true love? What do you feel when you dance with the one you love? Allow me to be a little bit cruel for a moment by saying that this is not happiness either.

If you are an older person, if you are not attracted to these pleasures, if they leave a bad taste in your mouth, forgive me if I tell you that it would be different if you were young and full of illusions.

At any rate, whatever you might say, parties or no parties, love or no love, whether you have that which is called money or not, you are not happy, although you might think the opposite.

People spend a lifetime looking for happiness everywhere and die without ever finding it.

In America—and everywhere else in the world—there are many who hope to win the lottery some day; they think that this way they will find happiness. Some in fact do win. However, this does not bring them the happiness they yearn for so much.

When one is a young man, one dreams of the perfect woman, a princess from *One Thousand and One Arabian Nights,* someone extraordinary. Then the harsh reality of life hits: a wife and small children to support, difficult financial problems, etc.

There is no doubt that as the children grow so do the problems, and they might even become impossible to cope with... Naturally, as children get bigger, they need bigger shoes, which are more expensive. This is obvious. Naturally, as the children grow, their clothing is ever more costly. If you have money, this is not a problem; but if you don't, then it is a serious matter and there is a great deal of suffering involved.

Everything would be more or less bearable with a good wife, but if a man is betrayed, that is, if his wife cheats on him, then what is the use of him struggling to earn money for the household?

Unfortunately, there are extraordinary examples of wonderful women—true companions through both fortune and misfortune—but their husbands take them for granted, and worse still, abandon them for other women who will embitter their lives.

There are many young girls who dream of their prince. Unfortunately, the harsh reality is in fact different, and they end up marrying tyrants.

The greatest dream for a woman is to have a lovely home and be a mother—a blessed predestination. However, even if she marries a good man—which is unlikely—all things come to pass in the end. Sons and daughters get married and leave home or they are ungrateful to their parents. Ultimately, family life ends.

All in all, in this cruel world in which we live, there are no happy people... All the unfortunate human beings are unhappy.

In life we have met many individuals who are loaded with money and full of problems: they are involved in lawsuits, over-taxed, etc. They are not happy.

What is the use of being rich if one does not have good health? Wretched rich people! Sometimes they are more unfortunate than any beggar.

Everything passes in this life: things, people, ideas, etc. Those who have money and those who have none, also pass away. Nobody experiences genuine happiness!

Many people want to escape from themselves through drugs or alcohol. In truth, they not only fail to escape, but worse, they get trapped in an inferno of vice.

When an addict resolves to change his life, his friends (who were involved in alcohol, marijuana, or L.S.D.) disappear as if by magic.

Happiness is not achieved by running away from the me, myself, the ego. Instead, it would be interesting to grab the bull by the horns, to observe the "I," to study the "I," in order to discover the causes of suffering.

When one discovers the real cause of so much misery and bitterness, it becomes obvious that something can be done...

If we manage to eliminate our me, myself, our "I" of drinking sprees, our "I" of vices and our "I" of attachments that cause so much heartfelt sorrow within us; if we manage to eliminate those worries that torment our minds and make us ill, etc... then clearly what arrives is that which is timeless, that which is beyond the body, that which is beyond attachments and beyond the mind, that which is truly beyond our comprehension and is called happiness!

Unquestionably, while our consciousness remains trapped within the ego, the me, myself, the "I," in no way will be able to know genuine happiness.

Happiness has a quality that neither the me, myself, the "I," or the ego has ever known.

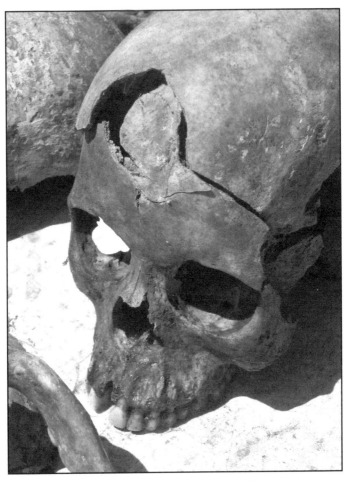

"Freedom, a lovely word, a beautiful
term; so many crimes have been
committed in its name!"

Chapter 4

Freedom

The meaning of freedom is something that has not yet been understood by humanity.

Always presented more or less erroneously, very serious mistakes have been made about the concept of freedom.

Certainly, we struggle for a word. We come to absurd conclusions; we commit all types of atrocities and shed blood on the battlefields.

The word freedom is fascinating, the whole world relishes it. Nevertheless, we have not grasped a real understanding of the term, and there is confusion regarding this word.

It is impossible to find a dozen people for whom the word freedom means the same thing, in the same way.

The term freedom will never be understandable by subjective rationalism.

Everyone has different ideas about this term; people's subjective opinions are totally devoid of objective reality.

When the question of freedom is propounded, in each mind there is incoherence, vagueness, and incongruity.

I am sure that even Immanuel Kant, author of *Critique of Pure Reason* and *Critique of Practical Reason*, never analyzed this word to find its exact meaning.

Freedom, a lovely word, a beautiful term: so many crimes have been committed in its name!

Unquestionably, the term freedom has hypnotized the masses. The mountains and valleys, the rivers and seas have been tainted with the blood conjured up by this magical word.

How many flags, how much blood, and how many heroes have come to pass in the course of history whenever the question of freedom has been posed in life's scenario?

Unfortunately, after achieving independence at such a high price, enslavement continues to exist within each of us.

Who is free? How many have attained this famous freedom? How many have been emancipated? Alas, alas, alas!

Adolescents long for freedom. It seems incredible that while having food, clothing, and shelter they should want to flee their homes in the pursuit of freedom.

It is incongruous that a teenage boy who has everything he needs at home is willing to run away, to escape from his abode, fascinated with the term freedom. Strangely, despite enjoying all the comforts of a happy home, he is ready to risk everything he has to travel the world and even come to grief. It is right that the pariahs in life, the outcasts of society, the poor should be eager to quit the slums and hovels in order to seek a change for the better. Yet, the spoiled child, the mama's boy, in search of a way out, is paradoxical and even an absurdity. However, this is how it is. The word freedom fascinates and enchants, although no one is able to define it precisely.

It is logical that a young girl wants freedom, longs to move away from home, to marry in order to escape from under the parental roof and lead a better life. This is in part due to her right to be a mother. Nevertheless, once married, she finds she is not free, and with resignation she must bear the shackles of slavery.

A worker, tired of so many regulations, wants to be free. Even if he achieves independence, he soon encounters the problem of continuing to be a slave to his own interests and concerns.

Certainly, each time that we fight for freedom we are disappointed, despite victory.

So much blood is shed pointlessly in the name of freedom while we continue to be slaves of ourselves and of others.

People fight for words they will never understand, although dictionaries give them the grammatical explanations.

Freedom is something that can only be achieved within ourselves. No one can achieve it outside of themselves.

"Riding through the air," is a very Eastern phrase which allegorizes the sense of genuine freedom.

No one can really experience freedom while their consciousness remains bottled up inside of the me, myself, the "I."

Understanding the myself, "my persona, what I am," is imperative if we sincerely wish to attain freedom.

There is no way we can destroy the fetters of our enslavement without previously and totally comprehending this question of "mine" and all that concerns the me, myself, the "I." What constitutes slavery? What is it that keeps us enslaved? What are the obstacles? We must discover all of this.

Rich and poor, believers and nonbelievers, all are actually prisoners, although they consider themselves to be free.

We will remain imprisoned, as long as the consciousness, the Essence, the most dignified and decent part within us, remains bottled up inside of the me, myself, the "I"—in our cravings and fears, in our desires and passions, our preoccupations and our violence, and in our psychological defects.

The sense of freedom can only be fully understood when we have annihilated the shackles of our very own psychological incarceration.

While the "I" exists, the consciousness remains imprisoned. Escaping from that prison is only possible through Buddhist Annihilation: dissolving the self, reducing it to ashes, to cosmic dust.

The liberated consciousness, devoid of the "I," absolutely absent of ego, without desires, without passions, without cravings and fears, directly experiences true freedom.

Any idea we might have about freedom is not freedom. Those opinions that we hold about freedom are far from reality. The ideas that we form on the subject of freedom have nothing to do with genuine freedom.

Freedom is something that has to be experienced directly, and that is only possible by dying psychologically, dissolving the "I," ending the me, myself forever.

It would do no good to continue dreaming about freedom if we continue being slaves.

It would be better to take a look at ourselves as we really are, carefully observing the fetters of slavery that keep us imprisoned.

Knowing ourselves, seeing what we are inside, we shall discover the door to authentic freedom.

Chapter 5

The Law of the Pendulum

To have a clock with a pendulum in the house is interesting, not only to check the time, but also as a source for some reflection.

Without its pendulum, this type of clock cannot function. The movement of the pendulum is profoundly significant.

In ancient times, the dogma of evolution did not exist. In those days, the sages understood that historical processes always take place according to the law of the pendulum.

Everything has its ebb and flow, its rise and fall, increase and decrease. Everything moves to and fro according to this marvelous law.

There is nothing strange about the fact that everything oscillates, is subject to the fluctuations of time, and that everything either evolves or devolves.

At one extreme of the pendulum lies joy, at the other lies sorrow. All our emotions, thoughts, longings, and desires swing according to the law of the pendulum.

Hope and desperation, pessimism and optimism, passion and misery, triumph and failure, profit and loss, surely correspond to the two extremes of pendular movement.

Egypt rose with all its power and majesty on the banks of a sacred river. But when the pendulum swayed to the opposite side, the country of the Pharaohs fell, and Jerusalem, beloved city of the Prophets, rose.

Israel fell when the pendulum changed position, and at the other extreme gave rise to the Roman Empire.

The movement of the pendulum raises and ruins empires, causing the ascent of powerful civilizations and later bringing about their destruction, etc.

The various pseudo-esoteric and pseudo-occultist schools, religions and sects can be placed at the right side of the pendulum.

The materialist schools—Marxism, atheism, skepticism, etc.—can be placed at the left side of the pendulum's movement. These are antitheses of pendular movement, changeable, subject to incessant permutation.

Because of some unusual event or delusion, a religious fanatic can move to the other extreme of the pendulum, changing to an atheist, a materialist, or a skeptic.

A materialistic, fanatical atheist can shift to the opposite extreme of the pendulum's motion and become an intolerable religious reactionary, due to some unexpected event. This could be due to a metaphysical or transcendental encounter, or to a moment of indescribable terror. For example, a priest defeated by the polemics of an esotericist, in desperation becomes incredulous and materialistic.

We knew of a case of a skeptical, atheistic woman who, because of a conclusive and definite metaphysical event, changed into a magnificent exponent of practical esotericism.

In the name of truth, we must declare that a true and absolute materialistic atheist is a farce, and nonexistent.

Faced with the proximity of inevitable death, faced with an instant of indescribable terror, the enemies of the Eternal One— the materialists and nonbelievers—go instantaneously to the other extreme of the pendulum. They resort to prayer, lamentation, and the clamor of infinite faith and enormous devotion.

Karl Marx himself, author of dialectical materialism, was a fanatically religious Jew who, after his death, was accorded the funeral rites of a chief Rabbi.

Karl Marx worked on his dialectical materialism with a sole purpose: To create a weapon in order to destroy all the religions of the world through skepticism.

This is a typical case of religious jealousy taken to the extreme. Marx could in no way accept the existence of other religions and preferred their destruction through his dialectics.

Karl Marx complied with one of the Protocols of Zion that literally stated:

KARL MARX

> "It is not important if we fill the world with materialism and repugnant atheism. The day when we triumph we will disseminate the properly codified religion of Moses in a dialectical form and will not permit any other religions in the world."

It is interesting to note that in the former Soviet Union, religions were persecuted and the Soviet people were taught dialectical materialism. Meanwhile, the Talmud, the Bible, and religion were studied within the synagogues, and they operated freely with no problems at all. The leaders of the Soviet government were religious fanatics of the law of Moses, yet they poisoned the people with the farce of dialectical materialism.

We will never pass judgment against the people of Israel; we are only making a statement against certain elite double-dealers who pursue undisclosed ambitions. While poisoning the people with dialectical materialism, they secretly practice the religion of Moses.

Materialism and spiritualism, with all their resulting theories, prejudices, and preconceptions, are processed in the mind according to the law of the pendulum and are fashionable according to custom and time.

Spirit and matter are highly debatable—thorny concepts that no one understands.

The mind knows nothing of Spirit and nothing of matter.

A concept is nothing more than just a concept. Reality is not a concept, although we conceive many ideas about reality.

The Spirit is the Spirit (the Being) and is only recognized by Itself.

It is written: The Being is the Being, and the reason for the Being to be, is to be the Being Himself.

Fanatics of a material God, the scientists of dialectical materialism are 100 percent absurd empiricists. They talk of matter with dazzling and stupid self-sufficiency, when in fact they know nothing at all about it.

What is matter? Which one of those ignorant scientists knows? The question of so-called matter is a very touchy and highly disputable subject.

What is matter? Is it cotton? Iron? Flesh? Starch? Stone? Copper? A cloud? What is it? To decide that all is matter would be empirical and absurd, just as it would be absurd to assert that the whole human organism is a liver, or a heart, or a kidney. Obviously, each thing is what it is and everything else is something else; each organ is different and each substance is different as well. Therefore, which of all these substances is the ever hackneyed matter?

Many people play with concepts of the pendulum. However, concepts are not in fact reality.

The mind knows only illusory forms of nature but knows nothing of the truth contained within those forms.

Theories go out of fashion with time and the passing of the years. What one learns at school serves no purpose later. In conclusion, nobody knows anything.

Concepts of the extreme right or extreme left of the pendulum go out of date like women's fashion. They are all processes of the mind that take place on the surface of our understanding. They are nonsense, vanities of the intellect.

For any psychological discipline there is another opposing one. Any logically structured psychological process is opposed by another similar one. Nevertheless, what does it matter?

What interests us is what is real, the Truth. It is not a question of the pendulum. It is not found in the fluctuations of theories and beliefs.

Truth is the unknowable from instant to instant, from moment to moment.

Truth is found at the center of the pendulum—not at the extreme right, or at the extreme left.

When Jesus was asked, "What is truth?" He kept profoundly silent. And when the Buddha was asked the same question, he turned away and departed.

The Truth is not a question of opinions, of theories, or prejudices of the extreme right or the extreme left.

An idea about the Truth that the mind can form is never the Truth.

The idea which our understanding might have of Truth is never the Truth.

Any opinion we might have regarding Truth—however respectable it might seem—is in no way the Truth.

Neither spiritual trends nor their materialistic opponents can ever lead us to the Truth.

Truth is something that must be experienced directly, like getting burned when sticking our finger into the fire, or when we choke while gulping down water.

The center of the pendulum is found within ourselves, and it is there that we must directly discover and experience what is real, what is the Truth.

We need to explore ourselves directly in order to discover and profoundly know ourselves.

The experience of the Truth only comes when we have eliminated the undesirable elements, which together form the me, myself, the "I."

Truth comes only by eliminating error. Only by the disintegration of the myself—our mistakes, our prejudices and fears, our passions and desires, our beliefs and lusts, intellectual stubbornness and all types of self-sufficiency—does the experience of what is real come to us.

Truth has nothing to do with what has or has not been said, nor with what has or has not been written. It only comes to us when the ego has died.

The mind cannot seek the Truth because it does not know it. The mind cannot recognize the Truth because it has never seen it.

The Truth comes spontaneously to us when we eliminate all of those undesirable elements which form the me, myself, the "I."

As long as the consciousness remains bottled up in the me, myself, it will be unable to experience that which is real, that which lies beyond the body, beyond affections and the mind, that which is Truth.

When the myself is reduced to cosmic dust, the consciousness is liberated in order to finally awaken and experience the Truth directly.

The great Kabir Jesus rightly said:

> And ye shall know the truth, and the truth shall make you free. - John 8:32

What purpose does it serve for a person to know fifty thousand theories if he has never experienced the Truth?

Each person's intellectual system might be very respectable, but every system has its opponent, and not a single one is the Truth.

It is better to explore ourselves in order to gain self-knowledge so that one day we might directly experience what is real: that which is the Truth.

Chapter 6

Concept and Reality

Who or what can guarantee that concept and reality are exactly the same thing?

Concept is one thing and reality is another.

There is a tendency to overestimate our own concepts. It is almost impossible for reality to equal concept. Nevertheless, the mind, hypnotized by its very own concepts, always presumes that concept and reality are the same.

Any psychological process that is correctly structured using precise logic is opposed by a different one, strongly developed with similar or superior logic. Then what?

Two severely disciplined minds confined by ironclad intellectual structures argue with one another. They debate, in dispute over this or that fact of reality. Each believes its own concept to be exact and the other to be false. Which is right? Who can honestly guarantee either case? Which one shows that concept and reality are the same?

Unquestionably, each mind is a world of its own. In each and every one of us lies a kind of pretentious, dictatorial dogmatism that wants to make us believe in the absolute equality of concept and reality.

Nothing can guarantee absolute equality between concept and reality no matter how strong the structures of a line of reasoning might be.

Those who confine themselves to any logistical intellectual procedure are always inclined to make the reality of phenomena and the devised concepts agree. However, this is only the result of hallucinatory reasoning.

Being open to what is new is a difficult gift for the traditionalist. Unfortunately, people want to discover and discern their own prejudices, ideas, preconceptions, opinions, and theories in all natural phenomena. No one knows how to be receptive, to see what is new with a clear and spontaneous mind.

Let the phenomena itself speak to the sage; this should be logical. Unfortunately, sages of this day and age do not know how to view phenomena. They only want to see in them the confirmation of all their preconceptions.

Although it seems incredible, modern scientists know nothing about natural phenomena.

When we only perceive our own concepts in natural phenomena, surely, we are not seeing the phenomena itself but only our concepts.

Nevertheless, foolish scientists, amazed by their fascinating intellect, stupidly believe each of their concepts to be absolutely equal to this or that observed phenomenon, when the reality is different.

We do not deny that all those who are locked into this or that logistical procedure reject our assertions. Undoubtedly, the pontifical and dogmatic condition of the intellect would never be able to accept that any properly conceived concept does not coincide exactly with reality.

As soon as the mind observes any phenomenon through the senses, it rushes to immediately label that phenomenon with this or that scientific term. Unquestionably, this serves only as a patch to cover its own ignorance.

The mind does not really know how to be receptive to what is new. However, it does know how to invent highly complicated terminology with which it tries to classify—in a self-deceiving way—that of which it is surely ignorant.

Speaking now in a Socratic sense, we will say that not only is the mind ignorant, but even worse, it is ignorant of its ignorance.

The modern mind is terribly superficial. We have specialized in inventing extremely difficult terms to hide our own ignorance.

There are two types of science. The first is nothing more than a compost heap of subjective theories that abound out there; the second is the pure science of the great illuminati: the objective science of the Being.

Undoubtedly, it is not possible to penetrate the amphitheater of cosmic science without first dying within ourselves.

We must disintegrate all those undesirable elements that we carry within and which together form the "I" of psychology.

As long as the me, myself—our own subjective concepts and theories—continues to bottle up the superlative consciousness of the Being, it is absolutely impossible to directly comprehend the harsh reality of natural phenomena within us.

The Angel of Death has the key to nature's laboratory in his right hand. We can learn very little from the phenomenon of birth, but from death we can learn everything.

The unprofaned temple of pure science is found in the depths of the dark sepulcher.

If the seed does not die, the plant is not born. Only with death comes forth what is new.

When the ego dies, the consciousness awakens to see the reality of all of Nature's phenomena in and of themselves.

The consciousness knows that which it directly experiences for itself, the naked reality of life beyond the body, the affections, and the mind.

"We need to open ourselves so that the light
of consciousness can penetrate the terrible
darkness of the me, myself, the "I.""

Chapter 7

The Dialectic of Consciousness

In the esoteric work dealing with the elimination of the undesirable elements that we carry within, annoyance, weariness, and boredom sometimes emerge.

Without question, if we truly yearn for radical change we must always return to the original starting point and re-evaluate the basis of our psychological work.

To love the esoteric work is indispensable when we truly want a complete inner transformation.

Unless we love the psychological work that is conducive to change, the re-evaluation of principles becomes impossible.

It would be absurd to presume that we could be interested in the work if, in fact, we do not come to love that work.

This means that love is essential when, time and again, we attempt to reassess the basis for the psychological work.

Above all, it is urgent to know about that which we call consciousness, for there are many people who have never been interested in knowing anything about it.

Any ordinary person knows that when a boxer is knocked out in the ring, he loses consciousness. It is quite clear that when the unfortunate boxer comes to, he regains consciousness. Consequently, anyone can understand that there is a clear difference between personality and consciousness.

When we come into this world, all of us have three percent of our consciousness free. The other ninety-seven percent is divided into the subconsciousness, the infraconsciousness, and the unconsciousness.

The three percent of awakened consciousness can be increased as we work on ourselves.

It is not possible to increase consciousness by exclusively physical or mechanical procedures.

Undoubtedly, the consciousness can only awaken through conscious work and voluntary suffering.

Within us there are various types of energy which we must understand:

First, mechanical energy;

Second, vital energy;

Third, energy of the psyche;

Fourth, mental energy;

Fifth, energy of the will;

Sixth, energy of the consciousness;

Seventh, energy of the pure Spirit.

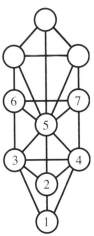

THE KABBALAH

No matter how much we might increase our strictly mechanical energy, we will never awaken consciousness.

No matter how much we might increase the vital forces within our own organism, we will never awaken consciousness.

Many psychological processes take place within us without any intervention from the consciousness.

However great the disciplines of the mind might be, mental energy can never achieve the awakening of the diverse functions of the consciousness.

Even if our willpower is multiplied infinitely, it can never bring about the awakening of the consciousness.

All these types of energy are graded into different levels and dimensions, which have nothing to do with the consciousness.

Consciousness can only be awakened through conscious work and upright efforts.

The minute percentage of consciousness that humanity possesses—instead of being increased—is usually wasted in life in a futile manner.

It is obvious that when we identify with all the events of our existence we are pointlessly squandering the energy of the consciousness.

We must view life as a film, without identifying ourselves with any comedy, drama, or tragedy, thus saving energy of the consciousness.

Consciousness itself is a type of energy with a very high frequency vibration.

We must not confuse consciousness with memory, which are as different from each other as are the headlights of a car from the road upon which we drive.

Many actions take place within us with no participation whatsoever of that which is called consciousness.

Many adjustments and readjustments take place within our organism without the participation of the consciousness.

The motor center of our body can drive a car, or direct the fingers that play piano keys, without even the most insignificant participation of the consciousness.

Consciousness is the light which the unconscious does not perceive.

A blind person does not perceive physical solar light either, but it does exist by itself.

We need to open ourselves so that the light of consciousness can penetrate the terrible darkness of the me, myself, the "I."

Now we can better understand the meaning of John's words when he said in the Gospel:

> And the light shineth in darkness; and the darkness comprehended it not. - John 1:5

But it would be impossible for the light of consciousness to penetrate within the darkness of the me, the myself if we have not previously used the marvelous sense of psychological self-observation.

We need to clear a path for the light to illuminate the terrible depths of the psychological "I."

We would never observe ourselves if we were not interested in changing. To be interested in changing is possible only when we truly love the esoteric teachings.

Now our readers will understand the reason why we recommend constant reevaluation of the instructions concerning the work on oneself.

Awakened consciousness allows us to experience reality directly.

Unfortunately, the intellectual animal—mistakenly called a human being—fascinated by the formulating power of dialectical logic, has forgotten about the dialectic of the consciousness.

Unquestionably, the power to formulate logical concepts certainly becomes terribly poor.

From thesis we go on to antithesis, and through discussion to synthesis, but the latter remains in itself an intellectual concept which can never coincide with reality.

The dialectic of consciousness is more direct, permitting us to experience the reality of any phenomenon in and of itself.

Natural phenomena never coincide exactly with concepts formulated by the mind.

Life unfolds from instant to instant, and when we capture it for analysis, we kill it.

When we try to infer concepts on observing this or that natural phenomenon, we in fact stop perceiving the reality of the phenomenon. We only see in that phenomenon the reflection of theories and stale concepts which have nothing at all to do with observed fact.

Intellectual delusion is fascinating and we want to force all natural phenomena to coincide with our dialectical logic.

The dialectic of consciousness is based on true life experiences and not on mere subjective rationalism.

All of Nature's laws exist within us, and if we do not discover them within, we will never discover them without.

The human being is contained in the universe and the universe is contained in the human being.

That which we experience within us is real. Only the consciousness can experience reality.

The language of the consciousness is symbolic, intimate, and profoundly significant. Only those who are awakened can understand.

Those who want to awaken consciousness must eliminate from within themselves all the undesirable elements that constitute the ego—the "I," the me, myself—within which the Essence is trapped.

"The body of any mutant violently challenges the
old texts of official anatomy."

Chapter 8
Scientific Jargon

Didactic logic is conditioned and qualified by the prepositions "on" and "about," which never take us to a direct experience of what is real.

Nature's phenomena are very far from being as scientists see them.

Certainly, as soon as a phenomenon is discovered, it is immediately qualified or labeled with this or that difficult term of scientific jargon.

Obviously, the difficult technology of modern science only serves as a cover for its ignorance.

Natural phenomena are in no way as scientists see them.

Life with all of its processes and phenomena unfolds from moment to moment, from instant to instant, and when the scientific mind detains it for analysis, it in fact kills it.

Any inference extracted from a natural phenomenon is in no manner equal to the concrete reality of that phenomenon. Unfortunately, the scientific mind, deluded by its own theories, firmly believes in the reality of its inferences.

A deluded intellect not only sees the reflection of its own concepts in phenomena. But also, and what is worse, it wants to dictatorially formulate phenomena to be exactly and absolutely equal to all those concepts carried in the intellect.

The phenomenon of intellectual delusion is fascinating. None of those ignorant, ultramodern scientists would admit the reality of their own delusions.

Certainly, the know-it-alls of our time would never allow themselves to be classified as deluded.

The power of their own autosuggestion has made them believe in the reality of all the ideas of scientific jargon.

Obviously a deluded mind presumes itself to be conscious and dictatorially wants all natural processes to march in step with its own pedantries.

As soon as a new phenomenon appears, we classify, label, and put it in place as though, in fact, we had understood it.

There are thousands of terms that have been invented to label phenomena, but the pseudo-sapient knows nothing of the reality of phenomena.

As a vivid example of everything that we are stating in this chapter we cite the human body.

In the name of truth we can affirm emphatically that the physical body is absolutely unknown to modern scientists.

Such an affirmation would appear to be very insolent to the pontiffs of modern science; unquestionably, in their eyes we deserve to be excommunicated.

Nevertheless, we have a very sound basis in which to make such a daring statement. Unfortunately, deluded minds are so convinced of their own pseudo-sapience that they could never even remotely accept the harsh reality of their ignorance.

If we were to tell the leaders of modern science that Count Cagliostro, a very interesting personage of the sixteenth, seventeenth, and eighteenth centuries, is still alive in the middle of this century; if we were to tell them that Paracelsus, the distinguished doctor of the Middle Ages, still exists today, you can be sure that the leaders of modern science would laugh at us and would never accept our affirmations.

However, it is so. They actually live on this Earth. They are genuine mutants, immortal men whose bodies date back thousands and even millions of years.

The author of this book knows mutants. However, he is aware of modern skepticism, the delusion of scientists and the ignorant state of know-it-alls.

Because of this, we are under no illusion that the fanatics of scientific jargon would ever accept the reality of our unusual statements.

The body of any mutant is an open challenge to the scientific jargon of our times.

The body of any mutant can change form and then return to its normal state without being damaged in any way.

The body of any mutant can penetrate instantaneously into the fourth dimension and assume any vegetable or animal form whatsoever, subsequently returning to its normal state without suffering any harm.

The body of any mutant violently challenges the old texts of official anatomy.

Unfortunately, none of these statements will convince those who are deluded by scientific jargon.

Those gentlemen, ensconced upon their pontifical thrones, unquestionably regard us with disdain, perhaps with anger, and possibly even with some pity.

However, the truth is what it is, and the reality of mutants is an open challenge to all ultramodern theory.

The author of this book knows mutants but expects no one to believe him.

Every organ in the human body is controlled by laws and forces, of which those deluded with scientific jargon, do not have even the faintest idea about.

Elements of Nature are in themselves unknown to official science. The best chemical formulas are incomplete: $H^2 0$, two atoms of hydrogen to one of oxygen to make water becomes something empirical.

If we attempt to join, under laboratory conditions, an atom of oxygen with two of hydrogen, the result is not water or anything like it, because the formula is incomplete; the element fire is missing. Only with this element (fire) is it possible to create water.

Intellectualism, no matter how brilliant it might seem, can never lead us to the experience of what is real.

The classification of substances and the difficult barbarisms with which we label them only serve as a cover for ignorance.

That the intellect wants this or that substance to have a specific name and certain characteristics is absurd and intolerable.

Why does the intellect presume itself to be omniscient? Why does it delude itself into believing that substances and phenomena are just the way it thinks that they are? Why does the intellect want Nature to be a perfect replica of all its theories, ideas, opinions, dogmas, biases and prejudices?

Indeed, natural phenomena are not as they are believed to be, and natural substances and forces are in no way as the intellect thinks they are.

The awakened consciousness is not the mind, the memory, or anything similar. Only liberated consciousness is capable of directly experiencing for itself the reality of life free in its motion.

However, we must emphatically affirm that as long as any subjective element exists within us, the consciousness will remain confined within such an element and, thus, will be unable to enjoy continuous and perfect enlightenment.

Chapter 9
The Antichrist

Dazzling intellectualism, as the manifested functionalism of the psychological "I," is without a doubt the Antichrist.

Those who suppose that the Antichrist is a strange personage born somewhere on the Earth or coming from this or that country are certainly completely mistaken.

We have emphatically stated that the Antichrist is definitely not a particular person, but all people.

Obviously, the Antichrist itself exists deep within each person and expresses itself in many ways.

Intellect which is placed in the service of the Spirit is useful; intellect which is divorced from the Spirit becomes useless.

Villains arise from intellectualism without spirituality: a vivid manifestation of the Antichrist.

Obviously, the villain, in and for itself, is the Antichrist. Unfortunately, the world today with all its tragedies and miseries is governed by the Antichrist.

The state of chaos in which modern humanity finds itself is undoubtedly due to the Antichrist.

The iniquitous one, of which Paul of Tarsus spoke in his Epistles, is certainly the harsh reality of our times.

The iniquitous one is already here. It manifests itself everywhere; it certainly has the gift of ubiquity.

It argues in cafés, negotiates at the United Nations, sits comfortably in Geneva, conducts experiments in laboratories, invents atomic bombs, remote-controlled missiles, asphyxiating gases, bacteriological bombs, etc...

The Antichrist, fascinated by its own intellectualism, which is absolutely exclusive to know-it-alls, believes that it knows all of the phenomena of Nature.

The Antichrist, believing itself to be omniscient, is trapped in the decay of its own theories. It directly rejects anything resembling God, or that which is worshipped.

The self-sufficiency, pride and arrogance of the Antichrist are unbearable.

The Antichrist mortally hates the Christian virtues of faith, patience, and humility.

Everyone bows before the Antichrist. Obviously, it has invented ultrasonic aircraft, wonderful ships, splendid cars, amazing medicines, etc.

Under such conditions, who can doubt the Antichrist? In this day and age, anyone who dares to speak against all the miracles and wonders of the Son of Perdition condemns himself to everyone's ridicule, sarcasm, and irony; he condemns himself to be classified as stupid and ignorant.

It is hard to make serious and studious people understand the former statements. They in and on themselves react and offer resistance.

Clearly, the intellectual animal mistakenly called human being is a robot, programmed at kindergarten, primary and secondary school, college and the university, etc.

No one can deny that a programmed robot functions according to its programming. In no way could it function if the program were removed.

The Antichrist has produced the program with which the humanoid robots of these decadent times are programmed.

Making these clarifications, emphasizing what I am saying, is frightfully difficult, as this is not in the program. No humanoid robot would admit things that are not in the program.

The absorption of the mind is so tremendous and serious a matter that a humanoid robot will never even remotely suspect that the program is useless; he has been organized according to that program and to doubt it seems like heresy, something incongruous and absurd.

For a robot to doubt its own program is absurd, an absolute impossibility, because its very existence depends upon that program.

Unfortunately, things are not as humanoid robots think they are. There is another science, another wisdom, which they find unacceptable.

The humanoid robot reacts, and rightly so, as it is not programmed to deal with another science or another culture, or anything else that differs from its well-known program.

The Antichrist has prepared the programs of the humanoid robot and the robot humbly prostrates itself before its master. How could a robot possibly doubt the wisdom of its master?

A child is born innocent and pure. The Essence expressing itself through each child is exceedingly precious.

Without a doubt, Nature deposits in the brain of newborns all the wild, natural, sylvan, cosmic, and spontaneous information indispensable for the capture or comprehension of truths. These are contained in any natural phenomena perceivable by the senses.

This means that a new born baby can discover by itself the reality of each natural phenomenon. Regrettably, the Antichrist's program interferes with it, and the marvelous qualities placed by Nature in the brains of the newborns are soon destroyed.

The Antichrist prohibits different ways of thinking; all babies that are born must be programmed by order of the Antichrist.

There is no doubt that the Antichrist mortally hates that precious sense of the Being known as the "faculty of instinctive perception of cosmic truths."

Pure science, different from the decaying university theories which exist here, there and everywhere, is something inadmissible for the Antichrist's robots.

Many wars, famines, and diseases have been propagated by the Antichrist throughout the world, and no doubt they will continue to be propagated before the arrival of the final catastrophe.

Unfortunately, the hour of the great apostasy has arrived (that time announced by all the prophets), and no human being will dare to rise up against the Antichrist.

Chapter 10

The Psychological I

This question of the me, myself, of what I am, of that which thinks, feels, and acts, is something that we must explore within ourselves in order for us to gain profound knowledge.

Everywhere there are lovely theories which attract and fascinate us. However, they are of no use at all if we do not know ourselves.

It is fascinating to study astronomy or to amuse ourselves somewhat reading serious works. Nevertheless, it is ironic to become erudite and not know anything about the me, myself, about the "I," about the human personality we possess.

Everyone is very free to think whatever they please and the subjective reasoning of the "intellectual animal"—mistakenly called a human being—can manage to do anything. Just as it can make a mountain out of a molehill, it can make a molehill out of a mountain. There are many intellectuals who constantly toy with rationalism, but in the end, what good does it do?

To be scholarly does not mean to be wise. Learned ignoramuses are as abundant as weeds. Not only do they not know, but they are not even aware they do not know.

Learned ignoramuses are those know-it-alls who believe they know everything and who indeed do not even know themselves.

We could theorize splendidly on the psychological I, but that is not exactly what interests us in this chapter.

We need to know ourselves directly as we are, without involving a depressing process of "options."

⅄ This would in no way be possible unless we were to observe ourselves in action from instant to instant, from moment to moment.

This is not a matter of seeing ourselves through theories or by simple intellectual speculation.

We are interested in seeing ourselves directly as we are; this is the only way we will be able to gain true knowledge of ourselves.

Although it might seem incredible, we are mistaken with regard to ourselves.

Many things we believe we have, we do not have, and many things that we do not believe we have, we do.

We have formed false concepts about ourselves, and we must, therefore, do an inventory to find out what we have too much of and what we lack.

We assume that we have such and such qualities, which indeed we do not, and we are surely ignorant of many virtues that we do possess.

✓ We are asleep, unconscious, and that is very serious. Unfortunately, we think the best of ourselves and never even suspect that we are asleep.

The Holy Scriptures insist on the need to awaken, but do not explain the system to achieve this awakening.

Worst of all, there are many who have read the Holy Scriptures and still do not understand that they are asleep.

Everyone believes that they know themselves and do not have even the faintest idea that there exists a Doctrine of the Many.

⌐ Indeed, each person's psychological "I" is multiple; it always consists of many.

By this we mean that we have many selves and not just one, as is always assumed by learned ignoramuses.

To deny the Doctrine of the Many is to make fools of ourselves. In fact, it is the height of absurdity to ignore the intimate contradictions which each of us possess.

"I am going to read a newspaper," says the "I" of intellect. "To heck with reading," exclaims the "I" of movement, "I prefer to ride my bicycle." "Forget it," shouts a third ego in disagreement, "I'd rather eat, I'm hungry."

If we could see ourselves in a full-length mirror, just as we are, we would discover for ourselves directly the Doctrine of the Many.

The human personality is only a marionette controlled by invisible strings.

The ego which swears eternal love for Gnosis is later replaced by another which has nothing to do with the pledge; then the individual leaves.

The "I" which swears eternal love for one woman is later replaced by another one which has nothing to do with that oath. Then the person falls in love with another woman, and like a house of cards it all collapses.

The "intellectual animal" mistakenly called human being is like a house filled with many people.

There is no order or agreement among the multiple I's; they all quarrel with each other and fight for supremacy. When one of them gains control of the capital centers of the organic machine, it feels unique, a master. Nevertheless, in the end it is overthrown.

Considering the matter from this point of view, we come to the logical conclusion that the "intellectual mammal" does not have a true sense of moral responsibility.

Undoubtedly, whatever the machine says or does at a given time depends exclusively on the type of ego in control at that moment.

It is said that Jesus of Nazareth drove out seven demons, seven egos, from the body of Mary Magdalene, living personifications of the seven capital sins.

Obviously, each of these seven demons is the head of a legion. Therefore, we can establish as a natural consequence that the intimate Christ was able to expel thousands of egos from the body of Mary Magdalene.

Reflecting upon all this we can clearly infer that the only worthwhile part of us is the Essence which, tragically, is trapped within these multiple I's of the revolutionary psychology.

Unfortunately, the Essence is always limited in its processes by virtue of its own imprisonment.

Without question the Essence—or consciousness, which is the same thing—sleeps deeply.

Chapter 11
Darkness

Certainly, one of the most difficult problems of our epoch stems from the intricate labyrinth of theories.

Undoubtedly, in these times there is an exorbitant multiplicity of pseudo-esoteric and pseudo-occultist schools here, there, and everywhere.

The marketing of souls, books and theories is frightening. Rare are those who really manage to find the Secret Path among the many cobwebs of contradictory ideas.

Gravest of all is intellectual fascination. There is a tendency to nourish ourselves only intellectually with all that reaches the mind.

The vagabonds of the intellect are no longer content with all the subjective literature and the ordinary types of books found in abundance in the bookstores. Now, to make matters worse, they also stuff themselves to the point of indigestion with cheap pseudo-esoterism and pseudo-occultism that abound everywhere like weeds.

The result of all this is a gibberish of confusion and manifest disorientation amongst the villains of the intellect.

I constantly receive all sorts of letters and books. Those who send them to me usually inquire about this or that school, this or that book. I confine myself to the following reply: "Refrain from idle mental curiosity. There is no need for you to be involved in other people's business. Disintegrate the animal ego of curiosity, for the business of other schools is not your concern. Become serious, know yourself, study yourself, observe yourself, etc."

Really, the important thing is to know ourselves profoundly in all mental levels.

Darkness is unconsciousness; light is consciousness. We must allow light to penetrate our own darkness; obviously, light has the power to defeat darkness.

Regrettably people find themselves incarcerated within the fetid, filthy environment of their own minds, worshipping their beloved ego.

People do not want to realize that they are not masters of their own lives. Indeed, each person is controlled from within by many other persons. I refer emphatically to the multiplicity of I's that we carry within.

Evidently, each one of these I's puts in our minds what we must think, in our mouths what we must say, and in our hearts what we must feel, etc.

Under such conditions the human personality is no more than a robot governed by different people, each disputing its superiority and aspiring to supreme control of the major centers of the organic machine.

In the name of truth, we solemnly affirm that the poor intellectual animal mistakenly called human being, though believing himself balanced, lives in a complete psychological imbalance.

The intellectual mammal is by no means unilateral, otherwise he would be balanced.

Unfortunately, the intellectual animal is multilateral, as has been proven repeatedly.

How can the rational humanoid be balanced? In order for perfect equilibrium to exist, we need an awakened consciousness.

Only the light of consciousness, directed not from different angles, but fully focused and centered upon ourselves, can put an end to the contrasts, to the psychological contradictions. Only thus can we establish within ourselves the true inner equilibrium.

The awakening of our consciousness will come if we dissolve the whole collection of I's that we carry within, thus the consequence or corollary will be the true balancing of our own psyche.

Unfortunately, people do not want to realize that they live unconsciously. They are deeply asleep.

If people were awake, each one of us would feel our fellow beings within ourselves.

If people were awake, our fellow beings would feel us within themselves.

Then, obviously, wars would not exist and the Earth would be, in truth, a paradise.

The light of consciousness endows us with true psychological balance and comes to establish each thing in its place. Anything that previously entered into intimate conflict with us, in fact, stays in its appropriate place.

The unconsciousness of the multitude is such that they are even unable to find the relationship existing between light and consciousness.

Unquestionably, light and consciousness are two aspects of the same thing. Where there is light, there is consciousness.

Unconsciousness is darkness, and the latter exists within us.

Only through psychological self-observation do we allow light to penetrate within our own darkness.

And the light shineth in darkness; and the darkness comprehended it not. - John 1:5

"Clearly, the Pharisees gather at their rites in
order to be seen, so that it will be said that
they are good people. They pretend in front of
others, but they never work on themselves."

Chapter 12
The Three Minds

Everywhere there are many scoundrels of the intellect lacking positive direction and who are poisoned with loathsome skepticism.

Certainly, the repugnant poison of skepticism has infected human minds alarmingly since the eighteenth century.

Before that time, the famous Nontrabada, or Encubierta island, located off the Spanish coast, was constantly visible and tangible.

There is no doubt that such an island is situated in the fourth dimension. Many are the anecdotes related to this mysterious island.

After the eighteenth century, the aforementioned island was lost in eternity; no one knows anything at all about it.

In the times of King Arthur and the Knights of the Round Table, elementals of Nature were manifest everywhere, deeply penetrating our physical atmosphere.

Many are the tales of elves, leprechauns, and fairies, which still abound in green Erin, Ireland. Unfortunately, all these things of innocence, all this beauty from the soul of the Earth is no longer perceived by humanity. This is due to the intellectual scoundrel's pedantries and the animal ego's excessive development.

Nowadays, the know-it-all ignoramuses laugh at all these things, rejecting them, though deep down they have not even remotely achieved happiness.

If people understood that we have three minds, it would be a very different story. They might even become more interested in these studies.

Unfortunately, learned ignoramuses, absorbed as they are in the labyrinth of their own difficult scholarly pursuits, do not even have the time to pay any serious attention to our studies.

These hopeless people are self-sufficient; they are conceited with vain intellectualism; they think that they are on the right path; and they do not have even the slightest idea that they are up a blind alley.

In the name of truth we must state that in synthesis we have three minds.

The first one we can and must call the **Sensual Mind**. The second we shall christen with the name of **Intermediate Mind**. The third we shall call the **Inner Mind**.

Now we are going to study each of these three minds separately and judiciously.

Unquestionably, the Sensual Mind develops its basic concepts via external sensory perceptions.

Under these conditions, the Sensual Mind is terribly crude and materialistic. It cannot accept anything which has not been physically demonstrated.

Since the fundamental concepts of the Sensual Mind are based on external sensory data, undoubtedly, it can know nothing about what is real, about the truth, about the mysteries of life and death, about the Soul and the Spirit, etc.

For the rogues of the intellect, totally trapped by their external senses and incarcerated within the basic concepts of the Sensual Mind, our esoteric studies are lunacy.

In the reasoning of the unreasonable, in an insane world, they are right, due to the conditioning by the external sensory world. How could the Sensual Mind accept what is not sensory?

If information from the senses serves as a secret means for all functions of the Sensual Mind, then it is obvious that the latter generates sensory concepts.

The Intermediate Mind is different. It has no direct knowledge of what is real either; it confines itself to belief and that is all.

Found in the Intermediate Mind are religious beliefs, unbreakable dogmas, etc.

The Inner Mind is fundamental for the direct experience of the truth.

Undoubtedly, the Inner Mind creates its basic concepts with information contributed by the superlative consciousness of the Being.

Unquestionably, the consciousness can live and experience reality. Without a doubt, the consciousness knows the truth.

To manifest itself however, the consciousness needs a mediator, an instrument of action, and this in itself is the Inner Mind.

Consciousness knows directly the reality of each natural phenomenon and can manifest it through the Inner Mind.

To open the Inner Mind would be the appropriate thing to do in order to remove ourselves from the world of doubt and ignorance.

This means that only by opening the Inner Mind will genuine faith be born within the human being.

Viewing this question from another angle, we would say that materialist skepticism is a characteristic peculiar to ignorance. There is no doubt that learned ignoramuses are 100 percent skeptical.

Faith is the direct perception of what is real, it is fundamental wisdom; it is the experience of that which is beyond the body, the affections and the mind.

We must distinguish between faith and belief. Beliefs are found stored in the Intermediate Mind. Faith is a characteristic of the Inner Mind.

Unfortunately, there is always a general tendency to confuse belief with faith. Although it seems paradoxical, we emphasize the following: "Those who have true faith do not need to believe."

This is because genuine faith is living knowledge, exact cognition, and direct experience.

For many centuries, people have confused faith and belief. Now it is very difficult to make them understand that faith is true knowledge and never futile beliefs.

The sapient function of the Inner Mind has as its intimate resource all that formidable data from the wisdom embodied in consciousness.

One who has opened the Inner Mind recalls one's previous existences, knows the mysteries of life and death; not because of what one has or has not read, not because of what someone has or has not said, not because of what one has or has not believed, but because of terribly real and vivid direct experience.

The Sensual Mind does not like what we are saying here. The Sensual Mind cannot accept this because it is out of its grasp, has nothing whatever to do with external sensory perceptions. This is alien to its own basic concepts, to that which was taught at school or what was learned from various books, etc.

What we are saying here is not accepted by the Intermediate Mind either, as it is contrary to its own beliefs. This spoils what its religious teachers made it learn by heart.

Jesus, the great Kabir, warned his disciples by saying:

> *Take heed and beware of the leaven of the Pharisees and the Sadducees.* - Matthew 16:6

Obviously, with this warning Jesus the Christ was referring to the doctrines of the materialistic Sadducees and the hypocritical Pharisees.

The doctrine of the Sadducees is the Sensual Mind. It is the doctrine of the five senses.

The doctrine of the Pharisees is irrefutably and without dispute situated in the Intermediate Mind.

Clearly, the Pharisees gather at their rites in order to be seen, so that it will be said that they are good people. They pretend in front of others, but they never work on themselves.

It is impossible to open the Inner Mind unless we learn to think psychologically.

Unquestionably, when someone starts to observe himself, it is a sign that he is beginning to think psychologically.

As long as we do not admit the reality of our own psychology and the possibility of changing it fundamentally, we certainly do not feel the necessity for psychological self-observation.

When one accepts the Doctrine of the Many Selves and understands the need to eliminate the different egos carried within one's psyche (for the purpose of liberating the consciousness, the Essence) undoubtedly, one initiates, in fact and by one's own rights, psychological self-observation.

Obviously, the elimination of undesirable elements carried in our psyches commences the opening of the Inner Mind.

All this means that the aforementioned opening takes place gradually as we annihilate those undesirable elements which we carry within our psyches.

Whosoever has eliminated those undesirable elements 100 percent from within, will also have obviously opened up the Inner Mind 100 percent.

Such a person will possess absolute faith. Now you will understand the words of Christ when he said:

> *If ye have faith as a grain of mustard seed, ye shall say unto this mountain, 'Remove hence to yonder place;' and it shall remove; and nothing shall be impossible unto you.* - Matthew 17: 20

"It pains one to see how people are born, grow,
reproduce like animals, suffer indescribably and
die without ever knowing why."

Chapter 13

Work Memory

Without a question, each person has his own particular psychology. This is indubitable, indisputable, and irrefutable.

Unfortunately, people never think about this, and many never accept it. This is because they are trapped within the sensorial mind.

Anyone would admit to the reality of the physical body since it can be seen and touched. Our psychology, however, is a different matter. It cannot be perceived by the five senses. For this reason we have a general tendency to reject or simply underestimate and scorn it, qualifying it as something of no importance.

Undoubtedly, when someone begins to self-observe, it is an unmistakable sign that they have accepted the tremendous reality of their own psychology.

Clearly, no one would attempt self-observation without having previously found a fundamental reason for doing so.

Obviously, someone who initiates self-observation becomes a very different person from others. This, in fact, indicates the possibility for change.

Unfortunately, people do not want to change; they are content with the state in which they live.

It pains one to see how people are born, grow, reproduce like animals, suffer indescribably and die without ever knowing why.

To change is fundamental but it is impossible if we do not initiate psychological self-observation.

We must start by seeing that our purpose is to acquire self knowledge, since rational humanoids really do not know themselves.

When one discovers a psychological defect, a great step has actually been taken, because this allows one to study and even radically eliminate that defect.

Indeed, we could not succeed in counting all of the psychological defects we have within since there are so many, not even if we had a steel palate and a thousand tongues to speak with.

Gravest of all is that we do not know how to measure the dreadful reality of any defect. We always look at it superficially without due attention. We see it as something unimportant.

When we accept the Doctrine of the Many Selves and understand the harsh reality of the seven demons that Jesus the Christ drove from the body of Mary Magdalene, obviously, our way of thinking (with regard to psychological defects) undergoes a fundamental change.

It cannot be asserted emphatically enough that the Doctrine of the Many Selves is 100 percent Tibetan and Gnostic in origin.

It is not at all pleasant to find out that within each person there lives hundreds and thousands of psychological people.

Each psychological defect is a different person existing within us, in the here and now.

The seven demons that the great Master Jesus the Christ threw out of the body of Mary Magdalene are the seven deadly sins: anger, greed, lust, envy, pride, laziness, and gluttony.

Naturally, each one of these demons leads separately to a legion.

In the Pharaohs' ancient Egypt, an Initiate had to eliminate the red demons of Seth from his inner nature if he wanted to achieve the awakening of consciousness.

Considering the reality of psychological defects, the aspirant longs for change. He does not want to continue in the state in which he lives with so many people within his psyche. He then begins self-observation.

As we progress in our inner work, we can verify for ourselves an interesting order in the system of elimination.

One is astonished when one discovers that there is an order in the work related to the elimination of the multiple psychic aggregates that personify our errors.

What is most interesting about all of this, is that such an order in the elimination of defects comes about gradually, and is processed according to the dialectic of consciousness.

The dialectic of reasoning will never surpass the formidable work of the dialectic of consciousness.

In time, the facts show us that the psychological order in the work of eliminating defects is established by our own profound inner Being.

We must clarify that a radical difference exists between the ego and the Being. The "I" can never establish an order in psychological matters as, in itself, it is the result of disorder.

Only the Being has the power to establish order in our psyche. The Being is the Being, and the reason for the Being to be is to be the Being Himself.

Order in the work of self-observation, judgment, and elimination of our psychic aggregates gradually becomes evident through the judicious sense of psychological self-observation.

All human beings have a sense of psychological self-observation in a latent state, but this sense develops gradually to the extent that we put it to use.

Such a sense allows us to perceive directly, and not through simple intellectual associations, the diverse selves that live within our psyches.

The question of extrasensory perception has begun to be studied in the field of parapsychology. In fact, it has been demonstrated in numerous experiments, prudently carried out over a period of time about which there is extensive documentation.

Those who deny the reality of extrasensory perception are utterly ignorant, villains of the intellect, incarcerated in the Sensual Mind.

Nevertheless, the sense of psychological self-observation is something that is deeper, which goes far beyond simple parapsychological conclusions. It allows us intimate self-observation and full verification of the terrible subjective reality of our diverse aggregates.

The establishment of a consecutive order of the different parts of the work related to this extremely serious subject of eliminating the psychic aggregates, allows us to generate a work memory. This is quite interesting, and even extremely useful in the question of inner development.

This work memory can certainly give us distinct psychological "photographs" of the different stages of our past. As a whole, it will bring to our imagination a vivid and even repugnant imprint of what we were before beginning the radical psycho-transforming work.

There is no doubt that we would never wish to return to that horrifying image, that vivid representation of what we once were.

From this point, such psychological "photography" is useful as a means of confrontation between a transformed present and a regressive, stale, clumsy and unfortunate past.

The work memory is always recorded on the basis of successive psychological events registered by the center of psychological self-observation.

In our psyche there are undesirable elements, the existence of which we do not suspect in the least.

For an honest man, honorable and worthy of respect, incapable of taking anything that does not belong to him, to unwillingly discover a series of thieving selves inhabiting the deepest regions of his own psyche is shocking... but not impossible.

A splendid wife, abundant in great virtues, or a maiden with exquisite spirituality and excellent education, may unwillingly discover through the sense of self-observation that groups of prostitutes live within her intimate psyche. Such a thought is sickening and unacceptable to any righteous citizen's intellectual center or moral sense. However, all of this is possible within the precise field of psychological self-observation.

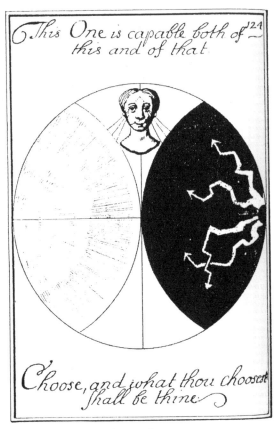

From Paradoxa Emblemata,
By D.A.Fraher, 18th century.

Chapter 14

Creative Comprehension

Being and knowing must be balanced to establish a sudden blaze of comprehension within our psyche.

When knowing is greater than being, it causes all kinds of intellectual confusion.

If being is greater than knowing, it can produce cases as serious as that of a stupid saint.

In everyday life, it is advisable to observe oneself with the purpose of self-discovery.

It is precisely everyday life, the psychological gymnasium, through which we can discover our defects.

In a state of alert perception, watchful attention, we can directly verify that the hidden defects flare-up spontaneously.

Clearly, we must work on the discovered defect consciously with the purpose of separating it from our psyche.

Above all, we must not identify with any I-defect if we really want to eliminate it.

Imagine that we are standing on a board and we wish to raise it to a position of it leaning against a wall. It would be impossible to do so if we were still standing on it.

Obviously, we must begin by separating the board from ourselves, removing ourselves from it and then lifting the board with our hands to a reclining position against the wall.

Similarly, we must not identify with any psychic aggregate if we truly wish to separate it from our psyche.

When one identifies with this or that I, one really strengthens, rather than disintegrates it.

Let us suppose that some lustful self took possession of any stereotypical image in the intellectual center to project lascivious and sexually morbid scenes on the screen of the mind. Unquestionably, identifying with the passionate picture greatly strengthens that lustful ego.

If, however, instead of identifying with such an entity, we separate it from our psyche, considering it as an intrusive demon, then obviously creative comprehension will have emerged within us.

Subsequently, we could have the luxury of analytically judging the aggregate in question with the purpose of becoming fully conscious of it.

The seriousness of the problem lies precisely with people's identification, and this is most regrettable.

If people were familiar with the Doctrine of the Many Selves, if they actually understood that not even their own lives belong to them, they would not make the mistake of identification.

Scenes of anger, pictures of jealousy, etc., in everyday life, are useful when we find ourselves in constant psychological self-observation.

Thus, we prove that neither our thoughts, nor our desires, nor our actions belong to us.

Unquestionably, multiple I's intervene like bearers of an ill omen, putting thoughts in our minds, emotions in our hearts and actions of all kinds in our motor center.

It is deplorable that we are not masters of ourselves and that various psychological entities make of us whatever they will.

Unfortunately, we do not even remotely suspect what is happening to us and we act like simple puppets, controlled by invisible strings.

Worst of all, instead of fighting for independence from all these secret tyrants, we make the mistake of fortifying them, and this occurs when we become identified.

Any street scene, any family drama, any silly quarrel between spouses is undoubtedly due to this or that I, and is something of which we must always be aware.

Everyday life is the psychological mirror in which we can see ourselves just as we are.

First, we must understand the need to see ourselves and the need to change radically. Only in this way will we want to really observe ourselves.

Whosoever is content with the state in which he lives, the foolish one, the dawdler, the negligent one, will never feel the desire to see himself; he will love himself too much to ever be willing to review his conduct and way of being.

We will say clearly that in some comedies, dramas and tragedies of everyday life various "I's" take part. These "I's" must be understood.

What comes into play in any scene of passionate jealousy are the egos of lust, anger, pride, jealousy, etc. We must later analytically judge each one separately to fully understand them with the clear purpose of their total disintegration.

Comprehension is very flexible, which is why it is necessary to delve deeper each time. What we understand in one way today we will better understand tomorrow.

Considering things from this angle, we can verify for ourselves how useful the diverse circumstances of life are when indeed we use them as a mirror for self-discovery.

We would never in any way attempt to say that the dramas, comedies and tragedies of everyday life are always splendid and perfect. Such a statement would be ludicrous.

Nonetheless, however absurd the different situations of existence may appear, they are marvelous as a psychological gymnasium.

The work relating to the dissolution of the diverse elements that form the me, myself, is terribly difficult.

Within the cadences of verse, misdeeds are also hidden. In the delightful perfume of the temples, transgressions lurk.

At times, crime becomes so sophisticated that people confuse it with sanctity, and so cruel that it eventually seems like sweetness.

Crime clothes itself in the judge's robe, the Master's tunic, the beggar's rags, the businessman's suit, and even in the habit of the Christ.

Comprehension is fundamental, but that is not all in the work of dissolving the psychic aggregates, as we shall see in the next chapter.

It is urgent, unavoidable and non-excludable that we make ourselves conscious of each ego, to separate each one from our psyche. But this is not all, something else is missing. For this we must see Chapter 15.

Chapter 15
The Kundalini

We have come to a very thorny point: I would like to refer to the question of the Kundalini, the igneous serpent of our magical powers mentioned in so many texts of oriental wisdom.

Without a doubt, the Kundalini has been well documented and it is something well worth investigating.

In texts of Medieval Alchemy, the Kundalini is the astral signature of the sacred sperm, Stella Maris, Virgin of the Sea, who wisely guides those who labor in the Great Work.

Among the Aztecs, she was known as Tonantzin, among the Greeks as chaste Diana. In Egypt she was Isis, the Divine Mother, whose veil no mortal has lifted.

There is no doubt at all that esoteric Christianity has never forsaken the worship of the Divine Mother Kundalini. Obviously she is Marah, or better said, RAM-IO, MARY.

What orthodox religions did not specify, at least with regard to the exoteric or public circle, is the aspect of Isis in her individual human form.

Clearly, it was taught only in secret to the Initiates that this Divine Mother exists individually within each human being.

It cannot be emphasized enough that Mother-God, Rhea, Cybele, Adonia, or whatever we wish to call her, is a variant of our own individual Being in the here and now.

Stated explicitly, each of us has our own particular, individual Divine Mother.

There are as many Mothers in heaven as there are beings who live on the face of the earth.

The Kundalini, an aspect of Brahma, is the mysterious energy that makes the world exist.

In her psychological aspect manifested in the hidden anatomy of human beings, the Kundalini is found coiled up

"The Divine Mother Kundalini has the power
to reduce any subjective and inhuman
psychic aggregate to ashes."

three and a half times within a certain magnetic center situated in the coccygeal bone.

There, resting numbly like any other snake, lies the Divine Princess.

In the center of that chakra, or abode, there is a female triangle, or yoni, wherein a male lingam is established.

In this atomic or magical lingam (which represents the creative sexual power of Brahma) the sublime serpent Kundalini is coiled up.

The igneous Queen, in her serpent form, awakens with the secretum secretorum of a certain alchemical craft which I have clearly taught in my book entitled *The Mystery of the Golden Blossom*.

Unquestionably, when this divine force awakens, it ascends victoriously up through the spinal medullar canal to develop powers of deification.

The sacred serpent, in its transcendental, divine, subliminal aspect, transcends the merely physiological and anatomical. In its ethnic state, it is as I have already said, our own Being, though derived.

It is not my purpose in this treatise to teach the techniques with which to awaken the sacred serpent.

I only wish to place certain emphasis on the harsh reality of the ego and the pressing inner need relating to the dissolution of its diverse inhuman elements.

The mind by itself cannot radically alter any psychological defect.

The mind can put a label on any defect, transfer it from one level to another, conceal it from ourselves or others, excuse it, etc., but never absolutely eliminate it.

Comprehension is a fundamental part, but it is not everything. Elimination is necessary.

An observed defect must be analyzed and understood completely before proceeding to eliminate it.

We need a power superior to the mind, a power capable of atomically disintegrating any I-defect which we have previously discovered and judged in depth.

Fortunately, such a power lies profoundly latent, beyond the body, the affections and the mind; although (as explained in previous paragraphs of this chapter), it has its actual exponents in the central bone of the coccyx.

After having fully understood any I-defect, we must submerge ourselves in profound meditation, imploring, praying, and asking our particular, individual Divine Mother to disintegrate the previously understood defect.

This is the precise technique required for the elimination of those undesirable elements that we carry within.

The Divine Mother Kundalini has the power to reduce any subjective and inhuman psychic aggregate to ashes.

Without this technique, without this procedure, all efforts to dissolve the ego are fruitless, pointless, and absurd.

Chapter 16

Intellectual Norms

In the course of everyday life, each person has his own criterion, a more or less stale way of thinking by not being open to new things. This is irrefutable, indisputable, and incontrovertible.

The mind of the intellectual humanoid is degenerate, deteriorated, and in an obvious state of devolution.

Indeed, the intellectual capacity for understanding of today's humanity is similar to that of an old, inert and absurd mechanical structure, itself incapable of any authentic flexible phenomena.

There is a lack of pliability in the mind. It is entrapped within various rigid and extemporaneous norms.

Everyone has their own rigid, fixed norms and criteria within which they incessantly act and react.

Most tragic of all in this matter is that millions of criteria equal millions of absurd and putrefying norms.

In any case, people never perceive themselves as mistaken; each mind is a world of its own, and there is no doubt that within so many mental labyrinths are found extensive deceitful sophisms and unbearable stupidity.

However, the narrow norm of the masses leaves no room for the slightest suspicion of the intellectual imprisonment in which it is found.

These modern people are pea brains who think the best of themselves, brag that they are liberals, super-geniuses, believe themselves to have a broad-minded approach.

Learned ignoramuses are the most stubborn ones. In reality, speaking Socratically this time, we would say: "Not only do they not know, but moreover they are unaware that they do not know."

The villains of the intellect cling to those antiquated standards of the past which are violently processed by virtue of their own imprisonment, and they emphatically refuse to accept anything which does not fit into their own cast-iron standards.

Learned know-it-all ignoramuses think that anything which, for one reason or another, departs from the rigid path of their rusty procedures is totally absurd. This is how these wretched people with their very difficult approach deceive themselves miserably.

Boasting of genius, the pseudo-sapient of this era look down in disdain at those who have the courage to withdraw from their decaying timeworn standards. Worst of all is that they do not even remotely suspect the harsh reality of their own crude awkwardness.

The intellectual wretchedness of those rancid minds is such that they even have the arrogance to demand demonstrations of that which is real, of that which is not of the mind.

People of stunted and intolerant intelligence refuse to understand that the experience of what is real comes only with the absence of the ego.

Unquestionably, it would be impossible to recognize directly the mysteries of life and death without opening the Inner Mind within us.

In this chapter, it would not be an overstatement to repeat that only the superlative consciousness of the Being can know the truth.

The Inner Mind can only function with information provided by the cosmic consciousness of the Being.

The subjective intellect, with its dialectical reasoning, can know nothing about what escapes its jurisdiction.

We already know that the concepts contained within dialectical reasoning are produced with information provided by the senses of external perception.

Those found to be imprisoned within their intellectual procedures and set standards will always offer resistance to these revolutionary ideas.

Only by the radical and definitive dissolution of the EGO is it possible to awaken the consciousness and actually open the Inner Mind.

Nevertheless, as these revolutionary statements do not fit into the confines of formal logic, or within dialectical logic, the subjective reactions of devolutionary minds raise violent resistance.

Those wretched intellectuals wish to pour an ocean into a glass, supposing that the university can control all the wisdom of the universe and that all cosmic laws are obliged to submit to their old academic rules.

The ignorant paragons of wisdom do not even remotely suspect the degenerate state in which they find themselves.

At times, such people stand out for a moment when they arrive in the esoteric world, but soon they are extinguished like will-o'-the-wisps, vanishing from the panorama of spiritual uneasiness, engulfed by intellect, disappearing from the stage forever.

The superficiality of the intellect can never penetrate the legitimate depths of the Being. However, subjective processes of rationalism can lead the foolish to all kinds of very brilliant conclusions, no matter how absurd.

Never can the formulating power of logical concepts imply the authentic experience of what is real.

The convincing game of dialectical reasoning causes the reasoner to be fascinated with himself so that he is always easily deceived.

The brilliant procession of ideas dazzles the scoundrel of the intellect and gives him a certain self-sufficiency so absurd that he rejects anything which does not smack of dust from libraries and ink of the universities.

Delirium tremens in a drunk alcoholic are an unmistakable symptom, but those intoxicated with theories are easily mistaken for geniuses.

Having come to this point in our chapter, we will state that it is certainly extremely difficult to know where the scoundrels' intellectualism ends and where their madness begins.

As long as we continue to be imprisoned within the corrupt and rancid norms of the intellect, it will be more than impossible to experience that which is not of the mind, that which is not of time, that which is real.

Chapter 17

The Knife of Consciousness

Some psychologists symbolize the consciousness as a knife very capable of separating us from that which is fastened to us, extracting our strength.

These psychologists believe that the only way to escape the power of this or that "I" is to observe it more clearly, each time with the objective of comprehending it so as to become cognizant of it.

These people think that in this way, separation of ourselves from this or that "I" will eventually occur, although it may be just by the width of a knife's edge.

In this manner, they say, the "I" separated by the consciousness resembles a cut plant. Becoming conscious of any "I," according to them, means separating it from our psyche and condemning it to death.

Without question, although apparently very convincing, such an idea fails in practice.

An "I" which has been cut off from our personality by the knife of consciousness, thrown out of the house like the black sheep of the family, continues in psychological space.

Transformed into a demon of temptation, it insists on returning home. It does not submit so easily. In no way does it wish to eat the bitter bread of exile. It looks for an opportunity, and when we let down our guard for a minute it accommodates itself anew within our psyche.

Gravest of all, is that within an exiled "I," there is always a certain percentage of Essence, consciousness, imprisoned.

All those psychologists who think this way have never been successful in dissolving any of their "I's"; they have actually failed.

No matter how hard one tries to evade the question of the Kundalini, it remains a very serious problem.

When the Serpent rises, it is Kundalini; when it descends, it is the abominable Kundabuffer organ.

And the LORD sent fiery serpents (the Kundabuffer) among the people (due to their own actions), and they bit the people; and much people of Israel died.

Therefore the people came to Moses, and said, We have sinned, for we have spoken against the LORD, and against thee; pray unto the LORD, that he take away the serpents from us. And Moses prayed for the people.

And the LORD said unto Moses, Make thee a fiery serpent (the Kundalini), and set it upon a pole: and it shall come to pass, that every one that is bitten (by Kundabuffer), when he looketh upon it (the Kundalini), shall live.

And Moses made a serpent of brass, and put it upon a pole, and it came to pass, that if a (Kundabuffer) serpent had bitten any man, when he beheld the serpent of brass (Kundalini), he lived.

- Numbers 21:6-9

In fact, the "ungrateful child" never progresses in the esoteric work on himself.

Obviously, an "ungrateful child" is anyone who scorns Isis, our own particular, individual, Divine Cosmic Mother.

Isis is one of the autonomous parts of our own Being, yet a derivative. The igneous serpent of our magical powers is Kundalini.

Obviously, only Isis has the absolute power to disintegrate any "I," this is irrefutable, indisputable and incontrovertible.

Kundalini is a compound word: KUNDA reminds us of the abominable "Kundabuffer organ," and LINI is an Atlantean term meaning termination.

Kundalini means "the termination of the abominable Kundabuffer organ." In this case, it is imperative not to confuse Kundalini with Kundabuffer.

As we already stated in a previous chapter, the igneous serpent of our magical powers is found coiled up three and a half times inside of a certain magnetic center located in the coccygeal bone at the base of the spinal column.

When the serpent rises, it is Kundalini; when it descends, it is the abominable Kundabuffer organ.

Through White Tantrism the serpent ascends victoriously along the spinal canal awakening the powers of deification.

Through Black Tantrism the serpent hurtles downward from the coccyx toward the atomic infernos of the human being. This is how many are transformed into terribly perverse demons.

Those who make the mistake of attributing all the sinister, negative characteristics of the descending serpent to the ascending serpent, definitely fail in the Work upon themselves.

The evil consequences of the abominable Kundabuffer organ can only be annihilated with the Kundalini.

It would not be an overstatement to say that such evil consequences are crystallized in the pluralized ego of revolutionary psychology.

The hypnotic power of the descending serpent has submerged humanity in unconsciousness.

By contrast, only the ascending serpent can awaken us. This truth is an axiom of Hermetic Wisdom. Now we better understand the deep significance of the sacred word Kundalini.

Conscious will is always represented as a sacred woman, Mary, Isis, who crushes the head of the descending serpent.

Frankly speaking, in plain language, the dual flow of light, the living and astral fire of the Earth has been represented in ancient mysteries as a serpent with a bull, billy goat, or dog's head.

It is the double serpent of the Caduceus of Mercury and the tempting serpent of Eden. But it is also, without the slightest doubt, the bronze serpent of Moses entwined in the "Tau," that is to say, the "generating lingam."

It is the male goat of the Sabbath and the Baphomet of Gnostic Templars, the Hyle of Universal Gnosticism, the double tail of the serpent that forms the feet of the Solar Cockerel of Abraxas.

The "black lingam" inserted in the metallic "yoni," (symbols of the God Shiva, of Hindustani divinity) is the secret key to awaken and develop the ascendant serpent or Kundalini. This is under the life long condition of never spilling the "vessel of Hermes Trismegistus," the thrice great God, Ibis of Thoth.

We have spoken between the lines for those who know how to understand. Whosoever has understanding let them understand, for herein lies wisdom.

Black Tantra practitioners are different. They awaken and develop the abominable Kundabuffer organ, serpent of temptation from Eden, when they commit the unpardonable crime of spilling the Sacred Wine during their rites.

Chapter 18

The Psychological Country

Unquestionably, just as there is an external country within which we live, there is also a psychological country within us.

People are never ignorant of the city or region within which they live. Unfortunately, the psychological place in which they are, is unknown to them.

At a particular point in time, anyone would know what neighborhood or community they are in. But psychologically speaking, it does not happen that way. Normally, people do not have the slightest idea of where they are in their psychological country, at any given moment.

Just as there are communities of decent, cultured people in the physical world, the same occurs in the psychological region within each one of us. Without a doubt, there are very graceful and beautiful communities within us.

Just as in the physical world, we have communities or neighborhoods with dangerous alleyways full of assailants, the same is true of the psychological regions within us.

It all depends on the type of person we associate with. If we have drunkards as friends, we will head for the pub, and if they are ultimately daredevils, undoubtedly our destiny will be the brothel.

Within our psychological country, each one of us has our own companions, our "I's" that will lead us where they need to, in keeping with their psychological characteristics.

A virtuous and honorable woman, a magnificent wife of exemplary conduct, living in a beautiful mansion in the physical world, might find herself within a den of prostitution (within her psychological country) because of her lewd "I's."

An honorable man of irreproachable honesty, a splendid citizen, could find himself in a den of thieves (within his psychological land) because of his vile companions, thieving "I's" deeply submerged within the subconsciousness.

"Within our psychological country, each
one of us has our own companions, our
"I's" that will lead us where they need
to, in keeping with their psychological
characteristics."

An anchorite and penitent, possibly a monk living austerely within his cell in a monastery, could find himself psychologically situated within a colony of murderers, gangsters, attackers and drug addicts. This is due precisely to the infraconscious or unconscious selves, profoundly submerged within the most complex labyrinths of his psyche.

There is a reason behind the saying, "There is much virtue in the wicked and much wickedness in the virtuous."

Many canonized saints still live within psychological brothels or dens of thievery.

That which we are affirming so emphatically may shock the sanctimonious, the pious, the learned ignoramuses and know-it-alls, but never the true psychologists.

Although it may seem incredible, in the incense of prayer, transgression is also hidden; in the cadences of verse, misconduct is also concealed; and beneath the sacred dome of the most holy sanctuary, crime drapes itself in the robes of sanctity and the sublime word.

Within the profound depths of the most venerable saints live "I's" of brothels, of theft, of homicide, etc.

They are the inhuman companions hidden in the bottomless depths of the subconsciousness.

Many have suffered for this reason; many saints throughout history. Let us remember the temptations of Saint Anthony and all the abominations against which our brother Francis of Assisi had to fight.

Nevertheless, not everything was revealed by those saints, and the majority of anchorites kept quiet in this regard.

It astonishes one to think that some of the most penitent and holy anchorites live in psychological communities of prostitution and thievery.

Still, they are saints, and if they have not yet discovered these frightening things within their psyches, when they do, they will quickly use cilices upon their flesh, and quite possibly will flail themselves. They will pray to their Divine Mother Kundalini to eliminate from their psyches these evil companions found in the dark caverns of their own psychological country.

Much has been said by the different religions about life after death and the great beyond.

Wretched people, they should not rack their brains anymore about what lies on the other side beyond the grave.

Without question, after death each of us continues living in our usual psychological community.

The robber will continue in the den of thieves; the lustful in the brothel will continue like a phantom of ill-omen; irritable, furious people will continue living in the dangerous alleyways of vice and anger where daggers gleam and gunshots ring out.

The Essence in itself is very beautiful. It came from above, from the stars. Lamentably, it is smothered deep within all these "I's" we carry inside.

By contrast, the Essence can retrace its steps, return to the point of origin, go back to the stars, but first it must liberate itself from its evil companions, who have trapped it within the slums of perdition.

When those distinguished Christified Masters, Francis of Assisi and Anthony of Padua, discovered within themselves the "I's" of perdition, they suffered terribly. There is no doubt that by means of conscious work and voluntary suffering, they succeeded in reducing to cosmic dust the assembly of inhuman elements that lived within them. Without a question, those Saints became Christified and returned to the point of origin after much suffering.

First of all, it is necessary, urgent and imperative that the magnetic center (which is abnormally established in our false personality) be transferred to the Essence. In this way, the complete human can initiate his journey from the personality up to the stars, ascending in a progressive, didactic way, step by step up the Mountain of the Being.

As long as the magnetic center continues to be established within our illusory personality, we will live in the most abominable psychological dens of iniquity, although appearing to be splendid citizens in everyday life.

Each of us is characterized by a magnetic center. The magnetic center of a merchant is in trade, and for this reason they are involved in the marketplace and attract those with whom they have an affinity: buyers and traders.

Scientists have in their personality the magnetic center of science, consequently attracting all scientific things: books, laboratories, etc.

The esotericist has the magnetic center of esoterism within. This type of center evolves differently in relation to the personality. Undoubtedly, for this reason transference occurs.

When the magnetic cnter is established in the consciousness, that is, in the Essence, then the complete human begins his return to the stars.

And Jesus asked him, saying, What is thy
name? And he said, Legion: because many
devils were entered into him.

- Luke 8:29-31

Chapter 19

Drugs

The human being's psychological split allows us to demonstrate the harsh reality of a superior level within each one of us.

When we have been able to verify, for ourselves, the concrete fact of two people within us, an inferior one on the ordinary, common, everyday level and a superior one at a higher octave, then everything changes. In this case, in life we endeavor to act according to the fundamental principles which we carry in the depths of our Being.

Just as there is an external life, there is also an internal life.

The external human being is not all there is; the psychological split teaches us the reality of the Inner Human Being.

The external human being has his own way of being. He is a thing of many activities and has typical reactions to life, a puppet operated by invisible strings.

The Internal Human Being is the genuine Being. His conduct is processed by other, very different laws, and he can never be transformed into a puppet.

The external human being does not make a stitch without a thimble; he feels poorly compensated; he feels sorry for himself; he is overly concerned with himself. If a soldier, he aspires to become a general; if a factory worker, he objects when he is not promoted; he wants due recognition for his merits, etc.

No one can reach the Second Birth, be reborn again (as it stated in the Gospel of the Lord), as long as they continue living with the psychology of the inferior, common, everyday humanoid.

When we recognize our own nothingness and internal misery, when we have the courage to review our life, undoubtedly we come to know for ourselves that in no way do we possess merit of any kind.

*Blessed are the poor in spirit, for theirs is the
kingdom of Heaven.*

The poor in spirit, or indigent of spirit, are actually those
who recognize their own nothingness, shame and inner misery.
This kind of being unquestionably receives Enlightenment.

*It is easier for a camel to pass through the eye of a
needle than for a rich man to enter the kingdom of
Heaven.*

It is obvious that the mind enriched by so many merits,
insignia and medals, distinguished social virtues and complicated academic theories is not poor in spirit, and thus could
never enter the kingdom of Heaven.

In order to enter the kingdom, the treasure of faith is
essential. As long as the psychological split has not been
produced within each of us, faith is more than impossible.

Faith is pure knowledge, direct experiential wisdom.

Faith has always been confused with vain beliefs; Gnostics
must never make such a serious mistake.

Faith is direct experience of the real, the magnificent vivifi-
cation of the Inner Human Being, authentic divine cognition.

The Inner Human being, by knowing his own internal
world through direct mystical experience, will obviously also
know the internal worlds of all the people who populate the
face of the Earth.

No one can perceive the internal worlds of the planet
Earth, the solar system, and the galaxy in which we live if we
have not previously come to know our own internal worlds.
This is similar to a person who commits suicide, who escapes
from life through a false door.

The extra-perceptions of a drug addict have their own
roots in the abominable Kundabuffer organ (the tempting
serpent of Eden).

The consciousness imprisoned within the multiple elements that constitute the ego is limited in its processes by
virtue of its own imprisonment.

Egoistic consciousness comes in a comatose state with hypnotic hallucinations very similar to those of someone under the influence of any drug.

We can present this matter in the following way: hallucinations from the egoistic consciousness are the same as hallucinations brought about by drugs.

It is obvious that these two types of hallucinations have their original causes in the abominable Kundabuffer organ (refer to chapter 17).

Obviously, drugs annihilate alpha waves. Then, unquestionably, the intrinsic connection between the mind and the brain is lost. This, in fact, results in total failure.

A drug addict turns vice into a religion. Being misled, he thinks he experiences what is real under the influence of drugs. Unaware that the extra-perceptions produced by marijuana, L.S.D., morphine, hallucinogenic mushrooms, cocaine, heroin, hashish, tranquilizers in excess, amphetamine, barbiturates, etc., are merely hallucinations produced by the abominable KUNDABUFFER organ.

Drug addicts devolve and degenerate in time. In the end they are submerged permanently within the infernal worlds.

"The Sun wants to create Human Beings."

Chapter 20
Inquietudes

There is no doubt that there is a big difference between thinking and feeling. This is indisputable.

Among people there is great indifference. This is the coldness of that, which has no importance, of that which is superficial.

The masses believe things of no importance to be important. They suppose that the latest fashion, the newest model car or the question of basic salary is the only serious matter.

They call "serious" the daily newspaper, a love affair, a sedentary life, a glass of alcohol, horse racing, bull fighting, car racing, gossip, slander, etc.

Obviously, when the modern human beings hear anything about esoterism, they respond with terrible coldness, or they simply sneer, shrug their shoulders and indifferently turn away. This is because it is not in their plans, it is not of interest within their social circles, nor is it sexually titillating enough.

This psychological apathy, this frightening coldness is based on two things: first, the most tremendous ignorance; second, the absolute absence of spiritual inquietudes.

A contact, an electric shock is needed. No one gave this to them at the store, nor was it found in what they believed to be serious, least of all, in the pleasures of bed.

If someone were capable of giving an electric shock to an indifferent imbecile or a superficial woman, a spark in the heart, some peculiar reminiscence, an inexplicable something that is all too personal, then perhaps everything would be different.

However, something displaces that secret voice, that initial hunch, that intimate yearning. This possibly could be a stupid triviality, a beautiful hat in some shop window, a delicious dessert at a restaurant, an encounter with a friend which later holds no importance for us, etc.

Trivialities and nonsense, while having no particular transcendence, still have the power at any given moment to extinguish that first spiritual disquietude, that intimate longing, that insignificant spark of light, that hunch which unsettles us for a moment without our knowing why.

If those who are currently living corpses, cold sleepwalkers in nightclubs or simply umbrella salespeople in department stores on the avenue, had not suffocated their initial intimate uneasiness, they would at this moment be spiritual luminaries, adepts of the light, real Humans in every sense of the word.

A spark, a hunch, a mysterious whisper, an unexplainable sensation felt sometimes by the butcher on the corner, by a shoe-shiner or a highly specialized doctor, is all in vain. The foolishness of the personality always extinguishes the primary spark of light, later continuing with a coldness of the most frightful indifference.

Unquestionably, people are swallowed up by the Moon sooner or later. This truth is indisputable.

There is no one, who at some point in his or her life has not felt an impulse, a strange disquietude. Unfortunately, anything from the personality, however stupid it may seem, is sufficient to reduce to cosmic dust that which, in the silence of the night, disturbs us for a moment.

The Moon always wins these battles; she feeds and nourishes herself precisely on our own weaknesses.

The Moon is terribly mechanical. Completely devoid of all Solar inquietudes, the lunar humanoid is incoherent and moves in a dream world.

If a person were to do what no one does (which is to revive the intimate uneasiness that arises, perhaps in the mystery of some night), there is no doubt that in the long run such a person would assimilate Solar Intelligence, and as a result would become a Solar Human Being.

This is precisely what the Sun[1] wishes; yet these ice-cold, apathetic and indifferent lunar shadows are always swallowed up by the Moon. Then comes the leveling of death.

Death levels everything. Any living corpse without Solar uneasiness gradually degenerates terribly until it is devoured by the Moon.

The Sun wants to create Human Beings. It performs these exercises in the laboratory of nature. Such experiments, unfortunately, have not produced good results; the Moon swallows up people.

Nonetheless, nobody is interested in what we are saying here, least of all the learned ignoramuses. They consider themselves to be mother hens or kings of the jungle.

The Sun has placed certain Solar seeds within the sexual glands of the intellectual animal (mistakenly called human being) which, when properly developed, can transform us into authentic Humans.

However, the Solar experiment is terribly difficult due precisely to lunar coldness.

People do not want to cooperate with the Sun and because of this the Solar seeds devolve, degenerate and are unfortunately lost in the long run.

The Master Key to the work of the Sun lies in the dissolution of the undesirable elements we carry within us.

When a human race loses all interest in Solar ideas, the Sun destroys it, because it serves no purpose in its experiment.

Since this present race has become unbearably lunar, terribly superficial and mechanical, it serves no further purpose for the Solar experiment: more than enough reason for its destruction.

In order for there to be continuous spiritual disquietude, it is necessary to transfer the magnetic center of gravity to the Essence, to the consciousness.

Unfortunately, people hold their magnetic center of gravity within the personality, in the cafe, in the canteen, in banking transactions, in brothels or the marketplace, etc.

[1 - The giver and supporter of life. A symbol of the Cosmic Christ, also known as Quetzalcoatl, Osiris-Ra, Apollo, etc.].

Obviously, all these belong to the personality, and the corresponding magnetic center attracts these things. This is incontrovertible, and anyone with any common sense can verify it directly for him or herself.

Regrettably, reading all of this, the scoundrels of intellect, accustomed as they are to constant argument or to remain silent with intolerable pride, prefer to throw away this book with scorn and read the newspaper.

A few sips of good coffee and the daily paper are splendid nourishment for rational mammals.

Nevertheless, they feel that they are very serious. Undoubtedly, their own pseudo-knowledge has deluded them, and the Solar matters written about in this insolent book offend them greatly. There is no doubt that the bohemian eyes of the homunculi of reasoning will not dare to continue with the study of this book.

Chapter 21
Meditation

In life, the only thing of importance is a radical, total and definitive change. The rest, frankly, is of no importance at all.

Meditation is fundamental when we sincerely yearn for such a change.

In no way do we want a type of meditation that is insignificant, superficial, and vain.

We must become serious and abandon the nonsense that abounds in cheap pseudo-esoterism and pseudo-occultism.

We must know how to take things seriously, how to change, if what we really and truly want is to not fail in the esoteric work.

Those who do not know how to meditate, the superficial, the ignorant, will never be able to dissolve the ego. They will always be impotent driftwood in the tumultuous sea of life.

Defects discovered in the field of everyday life must be understood profoundly through the technique of meditation.

The didactic material for meditation is found precisely in the different events and daily circumstances of everyday life. This is indisputable.

People always complain about unpleasant events. They never know how to see the usefulness of such events.

Instead of protesting against disagreeable circumstances, we must extract useful elements from them for our spiritual growth through meditation.

In-depth meditation on this or that pleasant or unpleasant circumstance allows us to savor the event and its outcome within ourselves.

It is essential to make a clear distinction between what it is to savor the work and what it is savor life.

In any case, to savor the work within ourselves requires a total inversion of the attitude with which we normally take on the circumstances of existence.

No one could savor the work while making the mistake of identifying with various events.

Certainly, identification impedes the proper psychological appreciation of events.

When someone becomes identified with this or that event, he will never be able to extract from those events the elements useful for self-discovery and inner growth of the consciousness.

The esoteric worker who reverts to identification after having let down his guard returns to savoring life instead of savoring the work.

This indicates that the previously inverted psychological attitude has returned to its state of identification.

Any unpleasant circumstance must be reconstructed through conscious imagination by means of the techniques of meditation.

The reconstruction of any event allows us to directly verify for ourselves the various "I's" participating in the event.

Let us take for an example a scene of jealous love in which the "I's" of anger, jealousy, and even hate intervene.

Understanding each of these selves, each of these factors, actually involves profound reflection, concentration and meditation.

The marked tendency to blame others is an obstruction, an obstacle to the understanding of our own mistakes.

Unfortunately, it is an extremely difficult task to destroy within ourselves the tendency to blame others.

In the name of truth, we would say that we are the only ones to blame for the diverse, unpleasant circumstances of life.

The different pleasant or unpleasant events exist with us or without us and are constantly repeated mechanically.

Based on this principle, no problem can have a final solution.

Problems are of life, and if there were a final solution, life would not be life, but death.

And so, there can be a modification of the circumstances and problems, but they will never stop being repeated, and there will never be a final solution.

Life is a wheel turning mechanically with ever recurring pleasant and unpleasant circumstances.

We cannot halt the wheel; good and bad circumstances always proceed mechanically; we can only change our attitude towards life's events.

As we learn to extract material for meditation from the very circumstances of existence, we will progress in our self-discovery.

Found in any pleasant or unpleasant circumstances are diverse "I's" which must be wholly understood with the technique of meditation.

This means that any group of selves which takes part in this or that drama, comedy or tragedy of everyday life, after having been totally understood, must be eliminated through the power of the Divine Mother Kundalini.

As we make use of the sense of psychological observation, it will also develop marvelously. Then we will be able to perceive the "I's" during the work of meditation.

It is interesting to perceive the "I's" internally, not only before they have been worked upon, but also throughout the duration of the work.

When these selves have been beheaded and disintegrated, we feel great relief and immense happiness.

*"Over millions of years, diverse characters
reunite to relive the same dramas, comedies
and tragedies."*

Chapter 22

Return and Recurrence

A human being is what his life is. If a human being does not work on his own life, he is wasting his time pitifully.

Only by eliminating the undesirable elements which we carry within us can we make a masterpiece of our life.

Death is the return to the beginning of life with the possibility of repeating it anew in the setting of another existence.

The various types of pseudo-esoteric and pseudo-occultist schools maintain the eternal theory of successive lives. Such a concept is mistaken.

Life is a film. Once the showing is over, we rewind the film on its reel and take it to eternity.

Re-entry exists, return exists. When we come back to this world, we project the same film, the same life on the screen of existence.

We can establish the thesis of successive existences but not of successive lives, because the film is the same.

Human beings have three percent free Essence, and the other ninety-seven percent is imprisoned within the "I's."

On return, the three percent of free Essence totally impregnates the fertilized ovum. Thus, unquestionably, we continue on in the seeds of our descendants.

Personality is different; there is no future for the personality of the deceased; it slowly dissolves in the mausoleum or cemetery.

In the newborn baby, only the small percentage of liberated Essence is reincorporated. This gives the child self-awareness and inner beauty.

The diverse selves, having returned, revolve around the newborn child, freely coming and going everywhere. They would like to enter the organic machine, however, this is not possible until a new personality has been created.

It is good to know that the personality is energetic, and that it is formed through experiences over time.

It is written that the personality is created during the first seven years of childhood, and that subsequently it is strengthened and fortified by all of the experiences of everyday life.

The "I's" start to intervene in the organic machine little by little as the new personality is created.

Death is a subtraction of fractions. Once the mathematical operation is terminated, the only things which continue are values, in other words, "I's" which are good or bad, useful or useless, positive or negative.

Values in astral light attract and repel one another according to the Laws of Universal Magnetization.

We are mathematical points in space which serve as vehicles for predetermined sums of values.

These values which serve as a basis for the Law of Recurrence are always found within our human personality.

Everything happens just as it happened before with the addition of the results or consequences of our former actions.

Since many "I's" from former lives exist within each one of us, we can emphatically assert that each of them is a different person.

This leads us to understand that within each of us lives a myriad of people, each with distinct commitments.

Within the personality of a thief exists a true den of thieves; within the personality of a murderer exists a gang of murderers; within the personality of a womanizer exists a bawdy house of lechers; within the personality of any prostitute exists a brothel, etc.

Every one of these people that we carry within our own personality has his or her own problems and commitments.

People living within people, persons living within persons, this is irrefutable, indisputable.

Gravest of all is that each of these persons, or selves, which live within us, comes from former existences and has set commitments.

The "I" that had a love affair at the age of thirty in a past existence will wait until that age in a new existence in order to manifest itself. When the moment arrives it will search for its dream lover and will telepathically contact the loved one. Finally the reencounter and reenactment of the scene will take place.

The "I" that at the age of forty was involved in litigation over property will wait in a new existence until that age in order to repeat the same course of action.

The "I" that at the age of twenty-five fought another man in a bar or pub will wait until that age in the new existence in order to seek out his adversary and repeat the tragedy.

The "I's" of one subject seek out those of another through telepathy, then reunite to mechanically repeat the same things.

This is actually the mechanism of the Law of Recurrence. This is the tragedy of life.

Over millions of years, diverse characters reunite to relive the same dramas, comedies, and tragedies.

A human person is no more than a machine at the service of those selves with so many commitments.

Worst of all, the commitments of these people within us are fulfilled without our prior knowledge or understanding.

In this sense, our human personality resembles a carriage being dragged along by many horses.

There are lives of the most precise repetition, existences which recur without any modification.

Life's comedies, dramas, and tragedies could never be repeated on the screen of existence if there were no actors.

The players in all of these scenes are the selves we carry within and which come from past existences.

If we disintegrate the "I's" of anger, the tragic scenes of violence will inevitably come to an end.

If we reduce the secret agents of greed to cosmic dust, problems stemming from them will stop completely.

If we annihilate the "I's" of lust, scenes of prostitution and sexual perversion will end.

If we reduce the hidden characters of envy to ashes, related events will radically terminate.

If we slay the "I's" of pride, vanity, conceit, and self-importance, the ridiculous scenes arising from these defects will draw to a close due to a lack of actors.

If we eliminate the factors of laziness, inertia, and negligence from our psyche, the horrifying scenes brought about by these types of defects will not be able to be repeated due to an absence of actors.

Feasting, drunkenness, etc., will come to an end for want of participants, if we pulverize the disgusting "I's" of voraciousness and gluttony.

Since these multiple selves are unfortunately processed at different levels of the Being, it becomes necessary to recognize their causes, their origins and the Christic procedures which will finally lead us to the death of the me, myself and to ultimate liberation.

The study of the Intimate Christ, the study of Christic esoterism is fundamental when we attempt to provoke a radical and definitive change within ourselves. This is what we will study in the following chapters.

Chapter 23

The Intimate Christ

Christ is the Fire of the fire, the Flame of the flame, the Astral Signature of fire.

Upon the cross of the martyr of Calvary, the mystery of Christ is defined in one word, consisting of four letters: INRI - *Ignis, Natura, Renovatur Integra - Fire Renews Nature Unceasingly.*

The Advent of Christ into the heart of the human being transforms us radically.

Christ is the Solar Logos, the Perfect Multiple Unity. Christ is life which beats throughout the entire universe. Christ is what is, what always has been, and what shall always be.

Much has been said about the Cosmic Drama; without a question, this drama is made up of four Gospels.

We have been told that the Cosmic Drama was brought to Earth by the Elohim. The great Lord of Atlantis acted out that drama in flesh and bone.

The great Kabir Jesus also had to play out the same drama publicly in the Holy Land.

Even if Christ were to be born a thousand times in Bethlehem, it would serve no purpose if he were not born within our hearts as well.

Although he died and was resurrected on the third day among the dead, this serves no purpose if he does not die and resurrect within our hearts as well.

To attempt to discover the nature and essence of fire is to try to discover God whose real presence has always been revealed secretly as an igneous aspect.

The burning bush (Exodus 3:2) and the fire at Sinai immediately after the issuances of the Decalogue (Exodus 19:18) are both manifestations in which God appeared to Moses.

Saint John describes the Master of the universe (Revelation 4: 3, 5) as one who had the appearance of jasper and sardine stone, the color of a flame, seated on an incandescent and shining Throne.

For our God is a consuming fire, writes Saint Paul in his Epistle to the Hebrews 12:29.

The Intimate Christ, the Heavenly Fire, must be born within us and, indeed, He is born when we have advanced sufficiently in the psychological work.

From our psychological nature, the Intimate Christ must eliminate the very causes of error, the Causal "I's."

As long as the Intimate Christ has not been born within us, the dissolution of the causes of the ego would not be possible.

The Living and Philosophical Fire, the Intimate Christ, is the Fire of the Fire, the Purest of the Pure.

Fire envelopes and bathes us totally; it comes to us through the air, through water, and through the earth itself. These are its preservers and its diverse vehicles.

The Heavenly Fire must crystallize within us. It is the Intimate Christ, our profound innermost Savior.

The Intimate Lord must take charge of our psyche, the five cylinders of the organic machine, all of our mental, emotional, motor, instinctual, and sexual processes.

Chapter 24

The Christic Work

The Intimate Christ emerges internally in the work related to the dissolution of the psychological self.

Obviously, the Innermost Christ only comes at the height of our deliberate efforts and voluntary sufferings.

The Advent of Christic Fire is the most important event of our own life.

The Intimate Christ then takes charge of all our mental, emotional, motor, instinctual, and sexual processes.

He is perfect, however, when he incarnates within us, He would appear to be imperfect. Being chaste, He would seem not to be chaste. Being just, it would appear as though He were not just.

This is similar to the different wavelengths of light. If we wear blue spectacles, everything appears blue, and if we wear red we see everything as that color.

Although He is white light, seen from the outside, each one of us will view Him through the psychological glass through which we are looking. For this reason, people looking at Him do not see Him.

Upon taking over all of our psychological processes, the Lord of Perfection suffers indescribably.

Transformed into a human among humans, he undergoes many trials and endures unspeakable temptations.

Temptation is fire. The triumph over temptation is Light.

The Initiate must learn to live dangerously, thus it is written. This is known by Alchemists.

The Initiate must travel, with determination, along the path of the razor's edge. There are terrifying abysses on either side of this difficult road.

On the difficult path to the dissolution of the ego, there are complex passages which have their roots precisely in the real path.

Obviously, from the path of the razor's edge multiple paths diverge which lead to nowhere. Some of them take us to the abyss and to despair.

There are paths which can transform us into the majesties of this or that zone of the universe. However, they can never return us to the bosom of the Eternal Universal Cosmic Father.

There are fascinating paths of a most holy, ineffable appearance; unfortunately, they can only lead us into the submerged devolution of the infernal worlds.

In the work of the dissolution of the "I," we need to devote ourselves completely to the Innermost Christ.

At times, problems appear which are difficult to resolve. Suddenly the path is lost in inexplicable labyrinths and we do not know where it continues. Only absolute obedience to the Innermost Christ and the Father who is in secret can, in such instances, wisely guide us.

The Path of the Razor's Edge is full of danger, both inside and out.

Conventional morals serve no purpose; morality is a slave to custom, time, and place.

What was moral in ages past is now immoral; what was moral in the Middle Ages, in these modem times, can be immoral; that which is considered moral in one country is immoral in another, etc.

In the work of the dissolution of the ego, it sometimes happens that when we think we are doing well, we are in fact doing badly.

Changes are essential during esoteric progress, but reactionary people remain trapped in the past, petrified in time, and they thunder and flash against us as we achieve deep psychological progress and radical changes.

People cannot bear the changes in an Initiate; they want him to continue to be petrified in many yesterdays.

Any change achieved by an Initiate is immediately classified as immoral.

Looking at things from this angle, in the light of the Christic Work, we can clearly prove the ineffectiveness of the diverse moral codes which have been written throughout the world.

Unquestionably, the Christ, manifested though hidden in the heart of the real human, once he takes charge of our diverse psychological states, is actually labeled as cruel, immoral and perverse because people do not know him.

It is paradoxical that although people worship the Christ, they classify him with such appalling labels.

Obviously, people who are unconscious and asleep only want an anthropomorphic, historic Christ of statues and unbreakable dogmas in whom they can easily fit all their clumsy, stale moral codes and all their prejudices and conditions.

People can never conceive of the Intimate Christ in the heart of the human being. The masses only worship the statue of Christ, that is all.

When one speaks to the multitudes, when one declares the harsh reality of the Revolutionary Christ to them, the Red Christ, the Rebel Christ, one is immediately labeled as the following: blasphemous, heretical, evil, profane, sacrilegious, etc.

Thus, the masses are always unconscious, forever asleep. Now we can understand why the crucified Christ on Golgotha exclaimed with all the strength of his soul, *Father forgive them, for they know not what they do.*

Christ himself being one, appears as many. This is why it is said that he is the Perfect Multiple Unity. *For whosoever knows, the Word gives power to. No one has uttered it, no one will utter it, except the one who has the Verb incarnated.*

To incarnate the Christ is vital in the advanced work of the pluralized "I."

The Lord of Perfection works within us as we consciously strive in the work upon ourselves.

The work which the Intimate Christ must do within our psyche is terrifyingly painful.

It is true that our Innermost Master must live through his way of the cross in the very depths of our own soul.

It is written, "Strike with thy rod while thou beg to thy God." It is also written, "Help thyself when thou art in thy greatest need, and God shalt assist thee."

To implore the Divine Mother Kundalini is fundamental when we attempt to dissolve undesirable psychic aggregates. However, the Intimate Christ, in the utmost depths of the myself, operates wisely in accordance with His own responsibilities which He, Himself has taken upon His shoulders.

Chapter 25

The Difficult Path

Unquestionably, a dark side exists within us which we neither know nor accept. We must carry the light of consciousness to this sinister side of ourselves.

The whole purpose of our Gnostic studies is to make the knowledge of ourselves more conscious.

When we have many things within ourselves which we do not know or accept, they complicate our lives dreadfully and, in fact, provoke all sorts of situations which could be avoided through knowledge of ourselves.

Worst of all is that we project this unknown and unconscious side of ourselves onto other people, and then we see it in them.

For example, we see others as liars, as unfaithful, miserly, etc., in relation to that which we carry within ourselves.

On this point, Gnosis says that we live in a very small part of ourselves. This means that our consciousness only extends to a very limited part of ourselves.

The idea of the Gnostic esoteric work is to clearly expand our own consciousness.

Undoubtedly, as long as we do not have a good relationship with ourselves we will not have good relationships with others, and the result will be all types of conflict.

It is essential to become much more aware of ourselves through direct self-observation.

A general Gnostic rule in the Gnostic esoteric work is that when we do have a point of contention with another person, we can be certain that this is the very thing against which we must work on within ourselves.

Whatever it is that we criticize so much in others is something which lies on the dark side of ourselves, and which we neither know nor want to recognize.

When we are in such a condition, the dark side of ourselves is very large, but when the light of self-observation illuminates this dark side, consciousness increases through self-knowledge.

This is the path of the razor's edge, more bitter than gall; many begin, very few reach the end.

Just as the Moon has a dark side which cannot be seen, an unknown side, the same is true of the Psychological Moon which we carry within.

Obviously, such a Psychological Moon is formed by the ego, the me, the myself, the "I."

In this Psychological Moon we carry inhuman elements which frighten and horrify, and which we would never accept that we have.

Such a cruel path is this one of the Innermost Self-realization of the Being. How many precipices! Such difficult steps! What horrible labyrinths!...

At times the inner path, after many twists and turns, hair-raising ascents and perilous descents, is lost in a desert of sand. One does not know where to continue and not one ray of light illuminates the way.

This is a path filled with dangers from within and without, a path of indescribable mysteries where only the breath of death blows.

On this inner path, when we think we are doing well, in fact we are doing badly.

On this inner path, when we think things are going badly, it happens that things are going well.

On this secret path, there are moments in which one neither knows what is good nor what is bad.

That which is normally prohibited, at times is that which is right; thus is the inner path.

All moral codes on the inner path are irrelevant; a beautiful maxim or a splendid moral precept could at certain moments become a very serious obstacle for the Innermost Self-realization of the Being.

Fortunately, the Intimate Christ, from within the very depths of our Being, works intensively, suffers, weeps, disintegrating very dangerous elements which we carry within us.

Christ is born as a child in the heart of the human being. However, as He eliminates the undesirable elements which we carry within, He grows little by little until He becomes a complete Human Being.

"The hidden Christ is Lord of the great
rebellion: the one who has been rejected by
the priests, by the elders and by the scribes
of the temple."

Chapter 26

The Three Traitors

In the profound inner work, within the sphere of the strictest psychological self-observation, we are to directly experience all of the cosmic drama.

The Intimate Christ has to eliminate all of the undesirable elements which we carry within.

The multiple psychic aggregates within our psychological depths scream for the crucifixion of the Innermost Lord.

Without a question, each of us carries three traitors within our psyches: Judas, the demon of desire; Pilate, the demon of the mind; and Caiaphas, the demon of evil will.

These three traitors crucify the Lord of Perfections in the very depths of our Soul.

This has to do with the three specific types of fundamental inhuman elements in the cosmic drama.

Without a doubt, this drama has always been endured secretly in the depths of the supreme consciousness of the Being.

The cosmic drama is not the exclusive property of the great Kabir Jesus, as is always supposed by learned ignoramuses.

Initiates throughout the ages, Masters of all times had to undergo the cosmic drama within themselves, in the here and now.

However, Jesus the great Kabir had the courage to perform such an intimate drama publicly, in the street, and in broad daylight. He did this in order to bring out into the open the significance of Initiation for all human beings, without distinction of race, sex, caste, or color.

It is wonderful that we have someone who publicly taught the innermost drama for all the people of the Earth.

Not being lustful, the Intimate Christ has to eliminate from within the psychological elements of lust.

Being in himself peace and love, the Intimate Christ must eliminate from within the undesirable elements of anger.

Not being covetous, the Intimate Christ must eliminate from within the undesirable elements of greed.

Not being envious, the Intimate Christ must eliminate from within the psychic aggregates of envy.

Having perfect humility, infinite modesty, being absolute simplicity, the Intimate Christ must eliminate from within the sickening elements of pride, vanity, and conceit.

The Intimate Christ, the Word, the Logos Creator, living always in constant activity must eliminate from within us, in Himself and by Himself, the undesirable elements of inertia, laziness and stagnation.

The Lord of Perfection, accustomed as he is to fasting, to moderation, never a friend of drunkenness and voraciousness, has to eliminate the abominable elements of gluttony.

A strange symbiosis is that of Christ-Jesus, the Human-Christ, that rare mixture of the divine and the human, of the perfect and the imperfect, an ever constant challenge for the Logos.

Most interesting of all is that the hidden Christ is always triumphant. He is someone who constantly vanquishes darkness, is someone who eliminates the darkness from within, in the here and now.

The hidden Christ is Lord of the great rebellion: the one who has been rejected by the priests, by the elders and by the scribes of the temple.

Priests hate him, that is, they do not comprehend him. They wish that the Lord of Perfection would live exclusively in time, according to their unbreakable dogmas.

The elders, that is, the Earth dwellers, good heads of households, sensible, judicious people, abhor the Logos, the Red Christ, the Christ of the great rebellion, because he is beyond their world of habits and antiquated, reactionary, petrified customs from so many yesterdays.

The scribes of the temple, the scoundrels of the intellect abhor the Intimate Christ because he is the antithesis of the Antichrist. He is the declared enemy of all the decaying university theories which abound so widely in the markets of bodies and souls.

The three traitors mortally hate the hidden Christ and lead him to death within us and within our psychological space.

Judas, the demon of desire always exchanges the Lord for thirty pieces of silver, or better said, for liquor, money, fame, vanity, fornication, adultery, etc.

Pilate, the demon of the mind, always washes his hands, always pleads not guilty, is never at fault, constantly justifies his actions to himself and to others, seeks excuses and loopholes in order to evade his own responsibilities, etc.

Caiaphas, the demon of evil will, unceasingly betrays the Lord within ourselves. The Intimate Adored One gives him the shepherd's staff to lead his sheep to pasture, but the cynical traitor converts the altar into a bed of pleasures, fornicates incessantly, commits adultery, sells the sacraments, etc.

These three traitors compel the adored Intimate Lord to suffer in secret without any compassion whatsoever.

Pilate forces him to put the crown of thorns upon his temples; evil "I's" scourge him, insult him, curse him in the innermost psychological space with no mercy of any kind.

"The Intimate Christ within us works with
intensity, eliminating all those hidden causes
of our errors through conscious work and
voluntary suffering."

Chapter 27

The Causal "I's"

The multiple subjective elements that form the ego have causal roots.

The Causal "I's" are linked to the laws of cause and effect. Obviously, there can be no cause without an effect, and no effect without a cause. This is unquestionable, indubitable.

Elimination of the diverse inhuman elements which we carry within would be inconceivable without the radical elimination of the intrinsic causes of our psychological defects.

Obviously, the Causal "I's" are closely related to specific karmic debts.

Only the most profound repentance and corresponding negotiations with the Masters of the Law can give us the joy of achieving disintegration of all those causal elements, which, in one form or another, can lead us to the final elimination of undesirable elements.

The intrinsic causes of our errors can certainly be eradicated from within us, thanks to the efficient work of the Intimate Christ.

Obviously, the Causal "I's" frequently have horribly difficult complexities. For example, a student of esoterism could be deceived by his instructor, and as a result that novice would become skeptical. In this concrete case, the Causal "I" which gave rise to such an error, could only be disintegrated through supreme inner repentance, and with very special esoteric negotiations.

The Intimate Christ within us works with intensity, eliminating all those hidden causes of our errors through conscious work and voluntary suffering.

The Lord of Perfection must live through the entire cosmic drama in our innermost depths.

One is astonished to contemplate all of the torture that the Lord of Perfection endures in the Causal World.

In the Causal World, the hidden Christ undergoes all the indescribable bitterness of his way of the cross.

There is no doubt that Pilate washes his hands and justifies himself, yet finally condemns the Beloved to death on the cross.

For the clairvoyant Initiate, the ascent to Calvary is extraordinary.

Indubitably, solar consciousness integrated with the Innermost Christ, crucified on the majestic cross of Calvary, utters terribly powerful phrases which human beings cannot comprehend.

The final phrase: *Father, into thy hands I commend my spirit* (Luke 23:46), is followed by thunder, lightening and great cataclysms.

Afterwards, when the nails are removed from his body, the Intimate Christ is placed in his Holy Sepulcher.

Thus, through death the Intimate Christ slays death. Then, much later in time, the Intimate Christ must resurrect within us.

Unquestionably, Christ's Resurrection radically transforms us.

Any Resurrected Master possesses extraordinary powers over fire, air, water, and earth.

Undoubtedly, Resurrected Masters acquire not only psychological, but also physical immortality.

Jesus the great Kabir still lives with the same physical body that he had in the Holy Land.

Count Saint Germain, who transformed lead into gold and made diamonds of the highest quality during the fifteenth, sixteenth, seventeenth, and eighteenth centuries, etc., still lives today.

The enigmatic and powerful Count Cagliostro—who astonished Europe so greatly with his powers during the sixteenth, seventeenth and eighteenth centuries—is a Resurrected Master and still exists with the same physical body.

Chapter 28

The Superman

One codex of Anahuac states that, "The Gods created humans of wood, and after having created them, fused them with divinity." But later adds, "Not all humans achieve integration with divinity."

Unquestionably, before integrating the human being with that which is the reality, what is first of all necessary is to create the Human Being.

The intellectual animal (mistakenly called a human being) is in no manner a Human Being.

If we compare a Human Being with the intellectual animal, then we can verify for ourselves the concrete fact that, although the intellectual animal physically resembles a Human Being, psychologically he is absolutely different.

Unfortunately, everyone thinks incorrectly, they presume they are Humans, qualifying themselves as such.

We have always believed that a Human Being is the king of creation. So far, the intellectual animal has not shown that he is even the king of himself. If he is not a king of his own psychological processes, if he cannot direct them at will, much less will he be able to govern Nature.

We cannot in any way accept a human being turned into a slave, incapable of governing himself, having been changed into a toy of the bestial forces of Nature.

Either we are kings of the universe or we are not. With reference to the latter, unquestionably, the concrete fact that we have not yet reached the state of a Human Being has been proven.

The Sun has deposited the seeds within the sexual glands of the intellectual animal in order to germinate a Human Being.

Obviously, such seeds can develop or be ultimately lost.

If we want those seeds to develop, it is essential to cooperate with the efforts that the Sun is making in order to create Humans.

An authentic Human Being must work intensively with the clear purpose of eliminating from within himself the undesirable elements which he carries inside.

If the real Human Being does not eliminate such elements from himself, he will then fail lamentably. He will become a miscarriage of the Cosmic Mother, a failure.

A Human Being who truly works on himself with the purpose of awakening consciousness can integrate with divinity.

Indeed, the Solar Human Being integrated with divinity is actually converted into a Super Human Being by his own right.

To become a Super Human Being, a Superman, is not easy. There is no doubt that the road which leads to the Superman is beyond good and evil.

A thing is good when it suits us and bad when it does not. Within the rhythms of poetry, crime is also concealed. There is much virtue in the villain and much evil in the virtuous.

The road which leads to the Superman is the path of the razor's edge. This path is filled with perils from both within and without.

Evil is dangerous and good is also dangerous. The frightening path is beyond good and evil; it is terribly cruel.

Any moral code can detain us on our way toward the SUPER-MAN. Attachments to such and such yesterdays, to such and such scenes, can halt us on the road which leads to the Superman.

However wise norms and procedures may be, they can obstruct us in our progress toward becoming a Superman if they are bottled up in this or that fanaticism, in this or that prejudice, or in this or that idea.

The Superman can distinguish good from evil and evil from good; he grasps the sword of cosmic justice and is beyond both good and evil.

The Superman, having liquidated within himself all good and evil values, has become someone whom nobody understands; he is the ray, the flame of the Universal Spirit of life, resplendent in the countenance of Moses.

In every refuge on the path, some anchorite gives his offerings to the SUPER-MAN, but the latter continues on his way beyond the good intentions of anchorites.

That which was spoken about by people beneath the sacred portals of the temples has great beauty; however, the Superman is beyond the pious sayings of people.

The Superman is the lightening and his word is the thunder which disintegrates the powers of good and evil.

The Superman shines in the darkness, but darkness hates the Superman.

The masses qualify the Superman as perverse for the very fact that he does not fit in with indisputable dogmas, neither within pious phrases, nor within the upright morality of serious people.

People abhor the Superman. They crucify him amongst criminals because they do not understand him, because they prejudge him, viewing him through the psychological lenses of what is believed to be holy, even if it is evil.

The Superman is like a flash of lightening which falls over the perverse, or like the brilliance of something which is not understood and which is later lost in mystery.

The Superman is not a saint, nor is he perverse; he is beyond sanctity and perversity. Nevertheless, people qualify him as holy or perverse.

The Superman glimmers for a moment within the darkness of this world and soon afterwards disappears forever.

Within the Superman, the Red Christ, the revolutionary Christ, the Lord of the great rebellion radiantly shines.

"Within this holy cup is the nectar of immortality, the Soma of the mystics, the supreme drink of the Holy Gods."

Chapter 29
The Holy Grail

The Holy Grail shines in the deep night of all the ages. During the Crusades, the Medieval Knights searched fruitlessly for the Holy Grail in the Holy Land, but they never found it.

When the prophet Abraham returned from war against the kings of Sodom and Gomorra, it is said that he encountered Melchizedeck, the Genie of the Earth. Certainly, this great Being dwelled in a fortress situated exactly in the place where, much later, Jerusalem, the city beloved by the Prophets was built.

Centuries of legend have it that Abraham celebrated the Gnostic Unction with the sharing of bread and wine in the presence of Melchizedeck. This is known to both divine and humans alike.

It would be worthwhile to say that at that time Abraham surrendered tithes and his first fruits to Melchizedeck, as is written in the book of the law.

Abraham received the Holy Grail from the hands of Melchizedeck. Much later in time, this goblet ended up in the temple of Jerusalem.

There is no doubt that the Queen of Sheba served as a mediator at this event. She appeared before King Solomon with the Holy Grail, and only after subjecting him to rigorous tests did she deliver unto him so precious a jewel.

The great Kabir Jesus drank from that goblet in the holy ceremony of the Last Supper, just as is written in the Four Gospels.

Joseph of Arimathaea filled the chalice with blood which flowed from the wounds of the Adored One on Mount Calvary.

When the Roman police searched the abode of this Senator, they did not find this precious jewel.

Not only did the Roman Senator hide this precious jewel in the ground, but he also kept with it the spear of Longinus with which the Roman centurion had pierced the side of the Lord.

Joseph of Arimathaea was incarcerated in a dreadful prison for not wanting to hand over the Holy Grail.

When said Senator was let out of jail, he went to Rome, taking the Holy Grail with him.

Arriving in Rome, Joseph of Arimathaea encountered the persecution of Christians by Nero, and he left by the shores of the Mediterranean.

One night while sleeping, an Angel appeared to him and said, "This chalice holds great power because within it can be found the blood of the Redeemer of the World." Joseph of Arimathaea, obeying the Angel's orders, buried the chalice in a temple located in Montserrat, in Cataluña, Spain.

With time, this chalice has become invisible, together with the temple and part of the mountain.

The Holy Grail is the vessel of Hermes, the cup of Solomon, the precious urn of all the temples of mysteries.

The Holy Grail was never missing from the Altar-stone of the Alliance, in the form of a cup or goblet within which was placed the manna from the desert.

The Holy Grail emphatically allegorizes the female yoni. Within this holy cup is the nectar of immortality, the Soma of the mystics, the supreme drink of the Holy Gods.

The Red Christ drinks from the Holy Grail at the supreme hour of Christification, so it is written in the Gospel of the Lord.

Never is the Holy Grail missing from the altar of the temple. Obviously, a priest must drink the wine of light from the sacred cup.

It would be absurd to imagine a temple of mysteries within which the blessed cup of all ages is missing.

This brings to mind Guinevere, the Queen of Jinn Knights, who poured wine into the delicious cups of SUFRA and MANTI for Lancelot.

Immortal Gods nourish themselves with the drink contained within the sacred cup; those who hate the blessed cup blaspheme against the Holy Spirit.

The Superman must nourish himself with the nectar of immortality, which is contained in the divine chalice of the temple.

Transmutation of the creative energy is fundamental when one wishes to drink from the sacred vessel.

The Red Christ, always revolutionary, always rebellious, always heroic, always triumphant, raises a toast to the Gods when drinking from the golden chalice.

Raise your cup aloft and take care not to spill even a drop of the precious wine.

Remember that our motto is *Thelema* (willpower).

From within the depths of the chalice (the symbolic figure of the female sexual organ) flames spring forth which blaze on the glowing face of the real human being.

Ineffable Gods of all the galaxies always drink of the nectar of immortality in the eternal chalice.

In time, the chill of the Moon brings about devolution. It is necessary to drink from the sacred wine of light in the Holy Vessel of Alchemy.

The purple of the sacred kings, the royal crown and flaming gold are only for the Red Christ.

The Lord of Lightning and Thunder grasps the Holy Grail in his right hand and drinks the wine of gold to nourish himself.

In fact, those who spill the vessel of Hermes during chemical copulation become sub-human creatures of the underworld.

Everything that has been written here can be found fully documented in my book entitled *The Perfect Matrimony*.

Index

Glorian Publishing is a non-profit publisher dedicated to spreading the sacred universal doctrine to suffering humanity. All of our works are made possible by the kindness and generosity of sponsors. If you would like to make a tax-deductible donation, you may send it to the address below, or visit our website for other alternatives. If you would like to sponsor the publication of a book, please contact us at 877-726-2359 or help@gnosticteachings.org.

Glorian Publishing
7420 SW Hunziker Rd Suite F
Portland, OR 97223 US
Phone: 877-726-2359 · Fax: 212-501-1676

VISIT US ONLINE AT:

glorian.info
gnosticbooks.org
gnosticteachings.org
gnosticradio.org
gnosticstore.org